Prayer Matters

reflections and suggestions for "doing prayer"

MARILYN WRAGG

ISBN 978-1-64079-809-0 (Paperback)
ISBN 978-1-64079-820-5 (Hard Cover)
ISBN 978-1-64079-810-6 (Digital)

Christian Faith Publishing, Inc.
296 Chestnut Street
Meadville, PA 16335
www.christianfaithpublishing.com

Printed in the United States of America

CONTENTS

Acknowledgment

To Mike, who loves, supports,
and prays with me each day

To Carolyn, Andy, Katie, Alexis, Charlie, and Miles,
who bring the joy of human love into my life
in each of your unique and precious ways

To David, whose joy in living and courage in dying
continually inspire me

To Rev. Paul Carpenter, who has led me to grow
exponentially through prayer and the Holy Spirit

To my First Christian Church family, Deborah sisters,
Bible study friends, and extended personal family
on earth and in Heaven, whose blessings in my life
will extend through Eternity

To God, to Whom all glory belongs

INTRODUCTION

I have a passion for prayer. I believe it is the most important thing we can do to experience personal peace and joy. It is also the most powerful thing we can do to help others. While praying is not a substitute for action, prayer has great power to undergird, guide, and greatly enhance the impact of our actions.

I have a passion for prayer, yet too often I neglect it. I have read many writings on prayer, yet I do not understand it. I have read all the Scriptures I can find that relate to prayer, yet I cannot explain it. I have implemented many and varied prayer practices, yet I am no closer to mastering the practice of prayer than a small child who is speaking to God out of the simplicity of the heart is.

Even so, I have, over the years, learned much about prayer. Others have said to me, "I know that prayer is your thing. But it's not mine." Friends, one thing I have learned is that we are all expected to pray. Jesus said so. In Matthew 6:5,

> **Prayer**: From Latin *precarius*—"obtained by entreaty;" from *precor*—"beg, entreat"

> "You can do more than pray after you have prayed, but you cannot do more than pray until you have prayed."
> *A. J. Gordon*

13

he said, "And **when** you pray…" In Luke 18:1, "Jesus told his disciples a parable to show them that they should always pray and not give up." The apostle Paul constantly modeled prayer, and in 1 Thessalonians 5:17, he admonished Christians to "Pray continually." From start to finish, the Bible is full of prayers and references to prayer.

> "For My thoughts are not your thoughts, neither are your ways My ways," declares the Lord. "As the heavens are higher than the earth, so are My ways higher than your ways and My thoughts than your thoughts." *Isaiah 55:8–9*

Another thing I have learned is that prayer is a mystery. There is no magic formula for prayer. There are Biblical principles that teach much about prayer, but God is God. He retains the right as to how and when He deems best to answer. Often, the answers are blessedly clear; sometimes, they are not. Just as God's ways are higher than our ways and His thoughts than ours, the ways and workings of prayer are quite beyond our current fathoming.

That does not mean we should be intimidated by or give up on prayer. Others have also said, "You are good at praying. I am not." Another thing I have learned is that we learn to pray by praying, just as we learn to walk by walking or to ride a bicycle by riding one. While it may come more naturally to some at first than others, anyone can learn. And the more we do it, the better we get at doing it.

That's what this book is about—doing prayer. It is a miscellaneous collection of insights and suggestions regarding various prayer matters that I have gleaned through exploring principles about prayer and through trying various ways to pray. It is the fruit of my entreating God to teach me to pray.

Although there is no prescribed pattern for reading and applying these prayer matters, I do suggest that you take time after reading each one to reflect on it for a while and apply it to your prayer life. Where a specific practice is suggested, try it for a period long enough to see how it works for you. And if it works for you, keep at it until it becomes a permanent part of your prayer repertoire. You may choose to linger over some practices for longer periods, while some you may skim through quickly.

Many selections are drawn from a series of prayer articles I have written for our church newsletter in the past few years. These happen to be years when I walked beside our son as he bravely battled cancer, and now as I grieve his passing to eternal life. Prayer, learning about it and doing it, has helped me throughout my life, but it has become my lifeline through these difficult years.

Because many people have told me that the articles were of great help to them, I have been led to expand and share them more broadly; hence this book. It is my prayer that it will provide readers with a few new insights and practices, which will lead to a deepening life of prayer, a more intimate relationship with God, and a more abundant life within the grace of Jesus Christ.

While there are many, many things I do not know about prayer and how it works, one thing I absolutely know for sure—**prayer matters!**

What the Bible Says About Prayer

Biblical teachings about prayer seemed to be a good way to set the stage for these prayer matters. However, when a search for Biblical references to prayer yielded over 400 results, the challenge became where to start.

Prayer is obviously important in the Scriptures. It is first mentioned early in the Bible, in Genesis 4:26: "That's when men and women began praying and worshiping in the name of God" (MSG). The last reference is Revelation 8:4: "The smoke of the incense, together with the prayers of God's people, went up before God from the angel's hand" (NIV*).

When you think about it, it is only natural that prayer is a key component from start to finish in the Bible. After all, the Bible tells the story of God's unfolding plan for a relationship with His children. When we are in a relationship with someone, we communicate with that person. Prayer is the way people throughout the Bible have communicated with God. There is much we can learn from Bible characters as we communicate with God through our individual prayers.

In the first three prayer matters, we will briefly look at what the Bible can teach us about the why, when, how, and what of prayer. The goal of these prayer matters, indeed of this entire collection, is that each of us will take away some new ideas to implement in our personal prayer lives so that we each may walk with God more closely as we grow as Christians.

* Note that all Scriptures referenced in this book will be the NIV version unless otherwise noted.

Prayer Matter 1

What the Bible Says About Prayer: Why Pray?

It is assumed in the Bible that the Lord's people pray to Him. Abraham, Isaac, and Jacob all practiced prayer. Moses fervently prayed ; Deuteronomy

> Lord, listen! Lord, forgive! Lord, hear and act!
> *Daniel 9:19a*

9:18 and 25 recorded his praying and fasting for 40 days on behalf of the Israelites. The kings and the prophets prayed; Daniel prayed; and Job prayed. Prayer permeates the Old Testament.

> While they were stoning him, Stephen prayed, "Lord Jesus, receive my spirit." *Acts 7:59*

In the New Testament are examples of prayers from characters such as Stephen, Peter, and John. Paul's epistles are filled with prayers of praise and petition. The most important examples are the numerous prayers of Jesus, who also directed his followers to pray.

> Then Jesus told his disciples a parable to show them that they should always pray and not give up. *Luke 18:1*

The bottom line is that if we love God and believe the Bible is true, prayer is a given. I suspect all Christians talk to God in our own ways and on our own schedules. However, from the Bible, we glean that those who have walked closely with God have made prayer the main business of their lives.

> "As it is the business of tailors to make clothes, and the business of cobblers to mend shoes, so it is the business of Christians to pray." *Martin Luther*

I suspect very few of us make prayer our main business, and there is much we can learn from the Bible about how to improve our communication with our God. As you read your Bible, be attuned to what the Bible says about prayer and, more importantly, how you can apply what it says to your own prayer life.

For personal reflection and action…

» Ask yourself, "Why do I pray?"
» Think of ways prayer has made a difference in your life this week.
» Ask God to help you make prayer the main business of your life.
» Take one step toward making prayer your main business.

Prayer Matter 2

What the Bible Says About
Prayer: Where and When?

"I want to learn about prayer. I know so little." In one sense, that statement is true for all of us, in that prayer is a practice you can spend a lifetime exploring, and yet, you always have more to learn. But, in another sense, we sometimes make prayer too hard. We may neglect it because we think we do not know enough about details such as when, where, and how.

Let's make it simpler. Prayer is communicating with God. So, stop and think about your interactions with the people you deeply love. How, when, and where do you communicate?

You probably communicate by whatever means is best at the moment. It may be one-on-one or in a group; it may be verbally, nonverbally, or in writing. Regarding when and where, it is usually whenever and wherever opportunities or needs arise. However, if a loved one is a long distance away or you are very busy, you need to schedule specific times or places to make sure you stay in touch.

Looking at Scriptural examples of prayer reveals that God's people communicated with Him in many times and places—in all the ways we communicate with loved ones. While the Bible does not give one specific formula, it does provide many ideas we can use in our own prayer lives. We certainly have much to learn from people who walked closely with God—most especially Jesus.

> Early in the morning, while it was still dark, Jesus got up, left the house and went off to a solitary place, where he prayed. *Mark 1:35*

> When Solomon finished prayers and supplications, he rose from before the altar of the Lord, where he had been kneeling with his hands spread out toward heaven. *1 Kings 8:54*

> Three times a day he (Daniel) got down on his knees and prayed. *Daniel 6:10b*

Solomon prayed at the altar in the temple.

Daniel prayed in his chamber, even after a law was passed that prohibited prayer under penalty of death.

Peter prayed on the roof.

> About noon… Peter went up on the roof to pray. *Acts 10:9*

From Scriptural glimpses, we learn that prayer was Jesus' lifeline with his Heavenly Father.

Jesus prayed morning and night. He prayed in deserted places and on mountainsides. He prayed whenever and wherever he encountered people in need.

> But Jesus often withdrew to lonely places and prayed. *Luke 5:16*

> One of those days Jesus went out to a mountainside to pray, and spent the night praying to God. *Luke 6:12*

Bible characters who earnestly sought God may have prayed in varied places, but they all made prayer a central component of their lives. For them, praying was a daily habit. Like Daniel, most followed the Jewish practice of praying three times each day.

While it is true that we can pray any time and at any place, the key question is, "Will we?" Let's make a commitment to learn from our Biblical role models and make prayer a central component of our lives.

For personal reflection and action…

» Think about when and where you prefer to pray.
» Recall when and where you have prayed over the past 24 hours.
» Prayerfully consider how you might pray more frequently or more regularly—perhaps adding additional times and places.
» Then, **do it!**

Prayer Matter 3

What the Bible Says About Jesus and Prayer

The Gospels show Jesus, who was raised as a devout Jew, praying often. For Jesus, prayer was a normal part of life. Prayer was his lifeline to God. He knew God as his Father, and he talked with his Father intimately and often. Jesus taught his disciples to follow his example. Through Scripture, which is alive and active today, he can likewise teach us. This prayer matter highlights a few principles and practices we learn from studying Jesus and prayer.

> For the word of God is alive and active. *Hebrews 4:12a*

> Jesus often withdrew to lonely places and prayed. *Luke 5:16*

Jesus often prayed by himself. He understood the need to spend time alone with God. Our relationship with our Heavenly Father is personal, and growing in that relationship requires time alone with Him.

Jesus also prayed with others. It was after praying in the company of his disciples that they asked Jesus to teach them to pray. Acts 1:14 confirms the importance of Christians praying with one another. Praying with others is

> He took Peter, John, and James with him and went up onto a mountain to pray. *Luke 9:28b*

powerful. It draws us into a closer fellowship with God and one another.

> They all joined together constantly in prayer. *Acts 1:14a*

Jesus prayed in many different places. Mostly, he prayed wherever he was. But he also sought out places to pray where he could be alone with God, and those places frequently were in the solitude of nature. We also can pray wherever we are—in a car, at work, in church, on a walk, in the kitchen, on the golf course, in the beauty of nature, etc. Possibilities are endless, so look for times and places to pray that you might not have considered before.

Jesus taught that prayer does not require lots of words. The simple beauty of the Lord's Prayer in Matthew 6 is contrasted with the many words offered by hypocrites in the synagogues.

> When you pray, do not babble like pagans, who think they will be heard because of their many words. Do not be like them, for your Father knows what you need before you ask. *Matt. 6:7–8*

> "Be still and know that I am God." *Psalm 46:10a*

On the other hand, **Jesus also spent long periods of time in prayer**. He knew there were times and circumstances that called for extended time in prayer with his Heavenly Father. It may not take long to talk *to* God, but learning to talk *with* God requires time. It entails listening as well as speaking. It requires times of stillness and reflection. In times of sorrow or anguish, it takes time to rest in His loving arms and allow Him to grant comfort and peace.

> On one of those days, Jesus... spent the night praying to God. *Luke 6:12*

Jesus taught persistence in prayer. In his parables about the friend at midnight (*Luke 11:5–13*) and the persistent widow (*Luke 18:1–8*), Jesus taught his disciples to pray and not give up.

> Then Jesus told his disciples a parable to show them that they should always pray and not give up. *Luke 18:1*

When we are tempted to give up hope, when answers to prayer do not seem to be forthcoming, we should keep on praying.

For personal reflection and action…

» Compare your current prayer practices to those of Jesus. Select at least one practice to strengthen in your prayer life over the next two weeks. It may be praying alone more or praying with a partner. It may be practicing simpler prayers or resolving to pray for a longer period of time or perhaps in a new place. **Do it!**

» Think of a difficult circumstance where you struggle to keep on praying. Read the parables of Jesus referenced above and resolve to pray and not give up. **Pray it!**

PRAYER MATTER 4

Find Your Prayer Closet

Although we see in the Bible examples of various times and places where God's people prayed, there is much to be said for having a special place for regular prayer. Jesus refers to such a place in his teachings about prayer.

In Matthew 6, Jesus instructs his followers not to pray for the purpose of receiving admiration from others. Rather, Jesus tells us to enter a private place, seclude ourselves, and pray secretly to our Father. Various Bible translations refer to the secluded place in this verse as a room, private room, inner chamber, or inner room.

"When you pray, do not be like the hypocrites. For they love to pray standing in the synagogues and on the street corners to be seen by men. Truly I say to you, they have their reward. But you, when you pray, enter your closet, and when you have shut your door, pray to your Father who is in secret. And your Father who sees in secret will reward you openly." *Matthew 6:5–6 (MEV)*

My first Bible, a King James translation, uses the term closet. I had to look up the definition of the word closet to get past picturing myself praying in the midst of hanging clothes. Our word closet is derived from Middle English or Old French and denotes a small, private enclosure or sequestered chamber.

I have come to treasure the term "prayer closet." My prayer closet is any special place where I go specifically to pray privately to my Father in Heaven. It has taken differing forms over my life.

When I was employed full-time, I would often close my office door at lunch to pray. Other times, weather permitting, I would take a walk on campus and find a secluded bench to sit and pray.

During our son's battle with cancer, I spent many weeks with him at Baylor Medical Center in Dallas. There, I located a prayer garden outdoors and an indoor chapel, which served as my away-from-home prayer closets for that season.

During that time and since David's death, I have used as my primary prayer closet a cozy nook I created by a secluded window in our home. It has a built-in window seat, with a cushion and pillows. My husband built a bookcase for my Bible and prayer items. The corkboard on the wall holds reminders of people and things to pray about.

Every morning, I enjoy devotional and prayer time at the kitchen table. And often, I am drawn outdoors to pray. But there is something about that nook, which I have restricted exclusively for prayer, that draws me quickly and deeply into God's presence. My prayer closet has become a place where I look forward to meeting and praying to my Father in secret. Surely, the peace and comfort I have received there, especially when most desperately needed, are but a small sampling of the reward Jesus promised in Matthew 6.

For personal reflection and action...

» Think about places that are most conducive to your praying. Consider places that are secluded and private, allowing you to pray "in secret."

» Designate your own private prayer closet.

» **Use it. Often.**

A Note of Clarification: Jesus was not saying in Matthew 6:5–6 that it is wrong ever to pray in front of others. What we are never to do is pray for the purpose of being rewarded by the praise of others. It is a question of what motivates our hearts, and that motivation should never be prideful. But there absolutely are times when it is appropriate—indeed, when we are called—to pray publicly, before small or large groups. In those times, our ability to pray effectively in public situations directly stems from the prayer life we have developed over much time spent in our private prayer closets.

PRAYER MATTER 5

Simple Prayer

There are many kinds of prayer and many ways to pray. Countless books have been written on the topic of prayer. In one sense, the multitude of prayer resources are blessings; yet in another sense, not so much. We may fail to grow in our prayer lives because, in light of all the information available, we think we just do not know enough about prayer. We think everything needs to

> Simple prayer is honest and uncomplicated. It is speaking to God from the heart, as a child to a parent.

be just right before we pray. Maybe we are angry or upset, and we don't want to present ourselves to God until we adjust our attitudes and lives.

That is where simple prayer can help us.

Simple prayer is pretty much coming to God as a child comes to a loving and trusted parent. We come just as we are, with no pretense. If we want something, we ask. If we are afraid, we admit it. If we are angry, we say so.

Children come to parents with all kinds of requests. Often, these requests are quite selfish, and sometimes there are complaints and demands for retribution. But the wise parent listens and is simply glad that the child comes to the parent—mixed motives and all.

Simple prayer is the most common form of prayer in the Bible. People like Moses and Jeremiah provide examples of inspired, noble prayers as well as prayers of complaint, frustration, and anger. The Psalms express varied emotions that range from love to graphic pleas for vengeance, from trust to self-pity.

So, when you find it hard to pray, for whatever reason—when you do not know how to begin—begin with, or revert to, simple prayer.

Begin wherever you are, just as you are. Pray about the ordinary events of life. Tell God about your joys as well as your sorrows. Share with Him your thanks as well as your complaints. Your Heavenly Father will receive you just as you are, and He will hear and receive your prayers just as you offer them.

> "Sometimes when your child talks, your friends cannot understand what he says; but the mother understands very well. So, if our prayer comes from the heart, God understands our language." *D. L. Moody*

Pray as Children

I desperately want my grandchildren to know God, and know Him well. To introduce them to prayer, I just said, "Prayer is how you talk to God." And so, they talk to God. Their prayers are simple and direct. Sometimes they praise God. They thank Him for all kinds of things—I mean *all* kinds of things. They ask Him for help when another child has been mean or when someone they know has problems.

During one evening prayer, instead of any of the above, my granddaughter told God at length about something that had happened that day. I was about to explain that this wasn't exactly a model of prayer, when Jesus' teaching about children popped clearly into my head along with a clear perception of God's delight at my granddaughter's sharing with Him.

Why pray? In simplest terms, it is because that's how we talk to God. The more we do it, the deeper our relationship with Him becomes. We start talking *with* God instead of just *to* Him. And that opens to us the Kingdom of Heaven right now, even as we live on planet Earth.

For personal reflection and action....

» Set aside one day this week when you make a point to talk to God throughout the day about whatever is going on at various moments. Tell God about how you feel—whether good or bad. Praise Him for blessings; share with Him your complaints, disappointments, and fears. At the end of the day, reflect on the experience.

» Determine how you might continue to talk more often with God about the daily business of life. **Ask** God to guide you in drawing closer to Him through simple prayer.

Prayer Matter 6

Use Your Voice

We have a dynamic pastor who, led by the Holy Spirit, has taught our congregation much about prayer. One of the simplest and most effective practices that Pastor Paul taught us is to "Use your voice."

Use your voice. In other words, pray out loud.

There have always been times when I have spoken aloud to God, but never had I done so with intent and frequency. I didn't think it necessary; after all, God hears our thoughts.

> I cried to the Lord with my voice, and He heard me from His holy hill. *Psalm 3:4 (NKJV)*

> I cried out to Him with my mouth; His praise was on my tongue. *Psalm 66:17*

Nevertheless, what Pastor Paul taught made sense, so I practiced using my voice. Once I started intentionally praying aloud whenever possible, the advantages of "using your voice" became obvious.

- Using your voice guards against distractions. Think how often you have been talking silently to God, only to realize your thoughts have gone in a totally different direction, or been praying in bed, only to realize later you drifted off to sleep. Contrast that with the likelihood of getting off track when you are speaking aloud, directly to someone. Certainly, you are unlikely to fall asleep.
- Speaking aloud helps you focus and clarifies thinking. Many thoughts can go through your mind at once, but you cannot speak them all at once. Talking out loud to God forces your mind to bring those thoughts into focus—to formulate what you want to say to your Heavenly Father.
- Using your voice feels much more like a "real" conversation than thoughts prayed silently in your mind. While it may feel awkward at first, speaking to God as if He were right there leads to greater intimacy with God as you more clearly grasp that, indeed, He **is** right there.
- Building on this growing sense of God's immediate presence enables you to pray with increasing sincerity and emotion. Psalms in the Bible express a vast array of human emotions, ranging from love, praise, and joy to anger, bitterness, and despair. I cannot imagine that the psalmists merely thought these expressions to God, but rather vocalized them with great emotion.
- Praying out loud gets you used to hearing your own voice when you pray. Then, when you pray aloud with a loved one or a friend or in a group setting, it is easier. You are already accustomed to using and to hearing your own voice.

- The desire to use your voice prompts you to locate prayer closets. Wanting to be alone so you can speak one-on-one aloud to your Father prompts you to begin to seek out places where you can pray privately.

There are obviously times when praying aloud is not an option. But, an added benefit of doing so as often as possible is that it trains you to pray more intently at all times. The more you use your voice, the more focused, "real," and emotive your prayers will become— whether you are praying aloud or silently.

For personal reflection and action…

» Beginning this week, take every opportunity to use your voice when praying.

» **Ask** God to guide and bless your efforts to speak more clearly and earnestly to Him.

» Look for places where you can be alone to pray out loud.

» Set aside times to go to those places and pray, using your voice.

» If it feels awkward or you do not know what to say, start with simple prayers.   Tell God about your day; thank God for your blessings and tell Him your worries. Read or recite a psalm, other Scriptures, or a favorite praise song or hymn.

» Stay the course. Keep using your voice until the practice becomes an effective boost to your prayer life.

Prayer Matter 7

Pray Immediately

Another prayer practice that our congregation quickly learned from Pastor Paul was to pray immediately. This he did not tell us with words; instead, he modeled it.

On one of his first days as our pastor, I rounded a corner and saw Paul holding hands and praying with a dear friend whose family member was critically ill. I quietly retreated for the moment. My friend told me afterward that in the course of introductions, her situation had come up; Paul had immediately said, "May I pray with

> And pray in the Spirit on all occasions with all kinds of prayers and requests. With this in mind, be alert and always keep on praying for all the Lord's people. *Ephesians 6:18*

> Do not be anxious about anything, but in every situation, by prayer and petition, with thanksgiving, present your requests to God. *Philippians 4:6*

you?" And he did, right then and there in the middle of the vacant hallway. She was deeply uplifted and touched.

In the weeks that followed, such instances became common occurrences as our new minister, very much led by the Holy Spirit and intent on becoming our pastor, prayed with individuals, church staff, church leaders, and all kinds of committees and groups. When a difficult situation was shared by anyone, Pastor Paul immediately stopped to pray with that person. If someone voiced a concern, the concern was lifted immediately in prayer, prior to discussing how it might be resolved.

> While walking with a friend to Sunday school class, she shared a deep concern. Where once I would have said, "I will pray for you," instead I asked, "Would you like to pray about that now?" She said, "Yes," and we stopped to pray right there. It was a powerful and moving experience.

Soon, many in our congregation were buzzing with excitement about this new openness to prayer, and many began to engage in immediate prayer. This simple practice has given my prayer life yet another power boost.

Often, I—and I suspect many of you—have responded to someone's

> An acquaintance called to tell me she could not meet me as planned because of a family crisis. Where once I would have said, "I will lift your family in my prayers," I instead said, "Can I pray with you over the phone?" Touched, she said, "Yes, please." We have since prayed often together.

sharing a deep need with, "I will pray for you." I always genuinely intend to pray, but many times I never get around to it, especially if it is a need that is not public or repeated to remind me to pray.

At other times, we even may say, "I will pray for you," because it sounds comforting and we do not know what else to say, when we never really intend actually to pray.

Praying immediately, as opposed to saying we will pray, has multiple benefits. It shows we are

> When I picked my young grandson up from school, he told me about a boy in his class who had gotten into a lot of trouble that day. It was obvious that my grandson felt compassion for the young boy and was sad. "Do you think we should pray for him?" "Yes, I would like that." We prayed together right then for God to help the boy through this and work the situation for good.

sincere in our promise to pray, and it keeps us from breaking that promise. It shows that we genuinely care and provides comfort. It creates a precious bond between the parties involved. It teaches us to pray on all occasions, in every situation, which grows our prayer lives. It ensures that the prayer of intercession is lifted up to God for the person, which is of utmost importance.

For personal reflection and action…

» **Ask** God to nudge you and guide you to practice immediate prayer.

» Be aware of opportunities to pray immediately. Times when you would otherwise say, "I will pray for you," are usually such opportunities.

» Graciously ask if you may pray with the individual. Some may say, "No." Of all the folks I have asked, only one has declined.

PRAYER MATTER 8

Bookend Each Day with Prayer

There is much to be said for solid beginnings and endings, from "A journey of a thousand miles begins with the first step," to "All's well that ends well."

> In the morning, O Lord, You hear my voice; in the morning I lay my requests before You and wait in expectation. *Psalm 5:3*

In life, we are given one day at a time. How we begin and end it can set the tone for how we live each day. And the sum total of all of those days adds up to how we live our lives. The psalmists have a solid prescription for effectively beginning and ending each day; do it with prayer. Start and end each day communicating with your Lord.

Bookend each day with prayer. On some days, your bookends may be lengthy, disciplined times of prayer in the morning and evening. On other days,

> On my bed I remember You; I think of You through the watches of the night. *Psalm 63:6*

they may be short, simple prayers. You might simply say at the start of your day, "Good morning, Lord. I love You. I turn this day over to You. Guide me by Your Spirit today." Your evening prayer might be, "Thank You for being with me this day. Forgive me for where I messed up; teach me how to do better tomorrow. Protect and refresh me through the night. Good night, Lord. I love You."

> And in the morning, rising up a great while before day, Jesus went out, and departed into a solitary place, and there prayed.
> *Mark 1:35 (KJV)*

Christ is the Alpha and the Omega, the beginning and the end. Make Him the beginning and the end of each day, and see the difference it makes.

Benefits of Morning Prayer

Through different seasons of life, I have experimented with praying at various times during the day. No matter what times I set for daily prayer, God blessed me with sharper focus, greater peace, and heightened sense of His presence on those days when I was faithful to adhere to my prayer times, regardless of when they occurred.

However, I have found over the years that, whenever else I may pray, taking time to pray first thing in the morning is vital. I also found the importance of morning prayer confirmed in Scriptures and by devotional writers.

Morning prayer sets the tone for the entire day. When your first focus has been on God, you see everything—whatever challenges that arise, whatever discouraging news you hear, whatever unexpected crises erupt—through the filter of God's love and sovereignty. When you begin by praying for God's Spirit to fill and guide you, you are equipped to face whatever the day may bring through God's power, not your own.

I rise before dawn and cry for help; I have put my hope in Your word. *Psalm 119:147*

> The Lord God ... awakens me each morning; He awakens my ear to listen like one being instructed. *Isaiah 50:4 (HCSB)*

For personal reflection and action...

» Work to develop the habit of starting and ending each day with prayer. Put a sticky note on your mirror, set a smartphone reminder, or whatever it takes to remind you to bookend your day with prayer.

» If there are mornings you oversleep or feel too rushed to take the time to pray, or evenings when you think you are too tired, at least stop, take a breath, and tell God "good morning" or "good-night." Thank your Father, and ask Him to be with you through the day and through the night.

PRAYER MATTER 9

The Secret of Being Content

I long for the mindset of the apostle Paul when he declared, "I have learned the secret of being content in any and every situation."

Contentment for me used to be a picture of settling in at home on an evening when I had no commitments, secure in the knowledge that my immediate loved ones were safe with me. That sentiment is reflected in the word, "cocooning," which was coined in the 1980s. Back in the 1960s, there was a song that similarly promised peace of mind through building a private world at home; I still recall the lyrics.

> "Cocooning"—building a cozy shell of perceived safety around one's loved ones in the private world of the family

Don't get me wrong: such cozy evenings can richly bless families and individuals, especially as the world gets crazier. However, the resulting peace of mind is fleeting. Causes for anxiety lurk at every corner, and we find all too soon that we do not have power to keep our loved ones safely cocooned.

So, we look to God's word for Paul's secret. We find in Philippians 4:12–13 that Paul had to **learn** to be content whatever the circumstance. As he grew in relationship with Christ, he learned to rely on Christ: "I can do all this through Christ who gives me strength." The key to Paul's growing relationship with Christ was prayer.

> I know what it is to be in need, and I know what it is to have plenty. **I have learned** the secret of being content in any and every situation, whether well fed or hungry, whether living in plenty or in want. I can do all this through him who gives me strength.
> *Philippians 4:12–13*

Earlier in the fourth chapter, Paul recommends powerful antidotes for anxiety—prayer and petition, with thanksgiving.

While *prayer* refers to a more general prayer of faith and *petition* (or *supplication*) to more specific pleas, the two overlap. Paul exhorted believers to come to God with "everything"—general requests, as well as the details that cause us anxiety.

And don't overlook *thanksgiving*. Research attests to the power of gratitude to combat fear and anxiety. When our prayers and petitions are sprinkled with thanksgiving to God, even our most dire needs

> Do not be anxious about anything, but in everything, by prayer and petition, with thanksgiving, present your requests to God. And the peace of God, which transcends all understanding, will guard your hearts and your minds in Christ Jesus.
> *Philippians 4:6–7*

take on a different perspective in light of "the riches of God's glory in Christ Jesus" *(Philippians 4:19)*.

> And my God will meet all your needs according to the riches of His glory in Christ Jesus. *Philippians 4:19*

Like Paul, each of us can learn to be content in any and every situation. The place to start is to live by Paul's inspired words in Philippians. In everything, pray.

For personal reflection and action...

"Paul's advice sounds great, but how do I actually do it?"

» The next time you find yourself fretting or worrying about something, shape those worries into prayers. Pause right then and tell God specifically what you are worried about. Ask that He enable you to turn your worries to Him *(1 Peter 5:7)*; then do your best to let it go. Remember to find something about the situation for which to thank God, or just thank Him for His power and presence.

» Remember, we have to **learn** such practices. So, when worries persist, do not give up. Keep practicing. Be sure to **ask God** to help you learn.

> Cast all your anxiety on Him because He cares for you. *1 Peter 5:7*

Prayer Matter 10

Pray to Pray

The four quotes cited in this prayer matter are from C. H. Spurgeon, a prolific British preacher and author during the late 1800s. They are powerful reminders that prayer is work, and the more we work at prayer, the more effective we become at praying.

Abraham's powerful intercession for Sodom, as recorded in Genesis 18, was built upon a lifetime of communing with God. The successful reign of King David was grounded in having one-on-one time with his Lord, as reflected in the many psalms written by this "man after God's own heart." The range of emotions

- "No doubt by praying we learn to pray, and the more we pray, the oftener we can pray."
- "Great power in prayer is within our reach, but we must go to work to obtain it."
- "Perseverance in prayer is necessary to prevalence in prayer."

expressed by David reflects the breadth and depth of his prayer life.

The ministry of Jesus was based upon continual and intense times of prayer with his Father, and Jesus taught his disciples to pray through example and teachings. The apostle Paul admonishes believers to pray continually and faithfully and on all occasions, and Paul models prayer throughout his epistles to the early churches.

> Pray continually...
> *1 Thessalonians 5:17*

Such Scriptures and quotes confirm the relationship between the frequency of our praying and the effectiveness of our prayers.

> Be joyful in hope, patient in affliction, and faithful in prayer.
> *Romans 12:12*

Spurgeon issued a wise warning: "He who prays in fits and starts is never likely to attain to that effectual, fervent prayer which availeth much." So, how do we attain this prayer that "availeth much"? According to Spurgeon, learn prayer by

> And pray in the Spirit on all occasions with all kinds of prayers and requests.
> *Ephesians 6:18a*

praying more. Persevere in prayer. Recognize prayer as the most important work we do. Commit to pray, and follow through.

Pray to Pray

> "We must **pray to pray**, and continue in prayer that our prayers may continue."

Spurgeon's advice, "We must **pray to pray**," can be applied in two ways. The first way, the principle that we learn to pray by praying more, is addressed above.

The second way is to pray specifically to be enabled to pray. In other words, ask God to increase your desire to pray and to help you pray more effectively.

For personal reflection and action…

» Reflect on these quotes and Scriptures about prayer.
» Invite God to give you a strong desire to pray often. Pray for God to help you find times to pray. **Ask** the Holy Spirit to nudge you to pray and give you strength to persevere in prayer.
» Practice praying on all occasions.
» Whenever you find your desire to pray waning, return to the intentional practice of asking God to draw you to pray.
» **Pray to pray!**

Prayer Matter 11

Pray Hymns

One night in October 2012, I woke up with my stomach churning in panic and my head spinning with fear. It took a moment's orientation to remember I was home in my own bed. For the previous weeks, I had been with our son David at Baylor Medical Center in Dallas. Following David's second stem-cell transplant, his wife and I had been taking turns living with him. I had just returned to Lubbock for a few days, leaving his wife—my dear daughter-in-law—with a very sick David.

David had valiantly fought Hodgkin's lymphoma for three years, maintaining his positive attitude and his love of life and family through very difficult circumstances. He had undergone numerous treatment cycles. Each treatment took an increasingly heavy toll on his body, but each time, David bounced back. So, in spite of tough odds, we prayed with great faith that this transplant would succeed in beating the cancer. But on day twenty-three, serious lung complications surfaced and things spiraled downhill. For the first time, the possibility that David might die became all too real, and I had dreaded leaving him for even these few days.

In the middle of that night, I slipped from my bed to my window-seat prayer closet. There, I cried and prayed. I begged God to take care of David, and I told Him how scared I was. I prayed desperately for a sign of God's encouragement. Finally, I was able to return to bed and sleep.

I awakened the next morning with words to the hymn "Great is Thy Faithfulness" playing in my mind. If you are not familiar with these beautiful lyrics, I suggest you look up or listen to the hymn.

> Through the Lord's mercies we are not consumed, for His compassions never fail. They are new every morning; great is Your faithfulness.
> *Lamentations 3:22–23*

> *Thank You, Father God, for Your great faithfulness. I pray that You will grant me strength for this day and bright hope for tomorrow. Let me never forget to count my many blessings, especially the blessing of Your dear presence. Thank You in advance for the new mercies that I will see each morning—even when times are hard—as I trust in You. I pray in the precious name of Jesus. Amen.*

I took that as God's sign of encouragement, given my state of mind when I had finally fallen asleep. Then, the Scripture for my morning devotional happened to be the Lamentations source for the hymn. When the closing church hymn the next day was "Great Is Thy Faithfulness," I wept at God's graciously providing me, in small but clear ways, the encouragement I so needed. The hymn continued to crop up for some time more often than could be attributed to chance. I turned the words into prayer and have prayed that hymn many times since.

God is creatively faithful in answering prayer. We can be creative in praying as well. Praying the hymns is one good way. Take the words to a favorite hymn and turn them into prayer. In any season of life, lyrics to great hymns and praise songs serve as additional sources of beautiful words for praising God. They are especially helpful in difficult seasons or whenever you find it hard to find the words to pray.

Through the ages, hymns have given expression to the faith of many. Try using them to express your faith and feelings to your Heavenly Father.

> God is creatively faithful in answering prayer. We can be creative in praying as well.

For personal reflection and action...

» Take selected lyrics from a favorite hymn or praise song. In your own words, turn the lyrics into prayer.

» **Ask** God to give you, or bring to mind, hymns that speak most meaningfully to you in each season of life.

» Watch for God's encouraging confirmation of this prayer practice!

Prayer Matter 12

Pray the 23rd Psalm

Psalm 23 is known and beloved by many, especially as a source of comfort in hard seasons of life. I have often prayed it for myself when I have been anxious or afraid or otherwise needed God's comfort. I simply reword the Scripture to

> The Lord is my shepherd; I shall not want. He makes me to lie down in green pastures; He leads me beside the still waters. He restores my soul; He leads me in the paths of righteousness for His name's sake.
>
> Yea, though I walk through the valley of the shadow of death, I will fear no evil;
>
> For You are with me; Your rod and Your staff, they comfort me. You prepare a table before me in the presence of my enemies; You anoint my head with oil; my cup runs over.
>
> Surely goodness and mercy shall follow me all the days of my life; and I will dwell in the house of the Lord forever. *Psalm 23 (NKJV)*

make it personal, starting with, "Lord, You are my shepherd; I trust in Your provision. Bless me with times of rest and refreshment..."

I have personalized it for loved ones by inserting their names throughout and customizing the principles expressed in each verse. "Lord, You are _____'s shepherd..."

I prayed it often as a blessing over my children as they grew up, and now I pray it for my grandchildren. I have prayed it for family members and friends who are in the hospital or other difficult circumstances.

Psalm 23 is a powerful prayer in any situation. But when, like the psalmist, you are literally walking in the shadow of death, it can enable you to pray when you cannot otherwise string words together. In the three weeks that followed the downturn in our son's condition, mentioned in the previ-

---

Lord, You are ___'s shepherd. Let him (or her) not want. Make ___ right now experience the peace of lying down in green pastures; lead him beside still waters. Restore his soul; lead him in paths of righteousness for Your name's sake. Though ___ walks through the valley of the shadow of death (or another challenge) let him not be afraid. Give him the strong assurance that You are with him; comfort him with Your rod and staff. Set Your promises before ___ like a banquet in the presence of everything that threatens him; anoint him with the oil of Your love. Make his cup overflow with blessings. Let Your goodness and mercy follow ___ all the days of his life. And grant him the strong assurance that he will dwell in Your house forever.

ous prayer matter, the 23rd Psalm became my go-to prayer. Nights were especially hard as David increasingly struggled. Psalm 23 prayers continually looped through my mind as I prayed for God to be with David, to comfort and protect my son, to give him rest and banish fear. My imagination took every promise of that psalm and turned it into word-pictures of prayer. I attribute my ability to remain calm and strong for David through those last weeks to God's leading me to pray those promises and then answering through His strong comfort and presence.

Whether praying in good times to bless dear ones or whether clinging for dear life to the words for yourself or a loved one in darkest times, you would be wise to memorize or to refresh your memory of Psalm 23. Practice turning it into prayer, and pray it often.

For personal reflection and action...

» Focus on the 23rd Psalm over the next weeks. Read it daily; try reading from different Bible translations. Reflect on the meaning of each phrase.

» Memorize Psalm 23 in the translation that speaks most personally to you. Recite it often, until it becomes soundly committed to memory.

» Phrase by phrase, turn the psalm into a prayer for yourself or someone else. **Ask** God to bring to mind those for whom you might pray. Pray it, often.

A Personal Postscript

Shortly before David died, he told me he had rememorized the 23rd Psalm when he entered the hospital that last time. Months later, it dawned on me that as God was moving me continually to pray this psalm over David, He was comforting David through the same verses. I claim that as assurance that the Lord was shepherding David every step through his last valley.

Prayer Matter 13

The Listening Side of Prayer

Prayer is conversing with our Heavenly Father. Conversing includes both speaking and listening. While there is much we need to learn and practice in order to speak well to God, speaking is by far the easier part of conversing. We've had lots of practice talking. We are not likely to be distracted when we are doing the talking. We are more in control of the talking side.

> "Listen and hear my voice; pay attention and hear what I say."
> *Isaiah 28:23*

The listening side is more difficult even in human interaction. It requires concentration, patience, and focus to process what we hear. It is easier to become distracted. We have less control on the listening side.

Now consider the challenges of conversing with our sovereign, Almighty, invisible God. It is not easy to talk well to God. How on earth can we listen well? How can we hear God speaking to us? How can we be sure it is God? How can we interpret what God is communicating to us?

I have a long way to go to listen well to God. But when I look back, I praise God that I have at least come a long way in learning to discern His voice.

The following are some suggestions that help me:

- **Petition God to teach you to listen.** First and foremost, remember that God is your Heavenly Father. He created you, He loves you, and He is reaching out to you. It is God Who has initiated the contact. Knowing that God wants you to hear

> "My sheep listen to my voice. I know them, and they follow Me." *John 10:27*

Him imparts confidence that He will help you do so if you earnestly try. Begin by asking God to show you how to listen, to teach you how to hear Him. Tell God you want to know Him better, so you can learn how to recognize His voice.

- **Expect God to respond.** Suppose a beloved child said to a wise and loving parent, "I realize I haven't been listening to you. Can you please show me how to listen so I can know what you want me to do?" Can you imagine how delighted that parent would be? Can you even imagine the parent not respond-

> "Call to Me and I will answer you and tell you great and unsearchable things you do not know." *Jeremiah 33:3*

ing? God is your Heavenly Father. He had a plan from the foundation of the world to reconcile you to Him through Jesus Christ so you can be in relationship with Him. Of course, He wants you to hear Him!

> Be still before the Lord, and wait patiently for Him.
> *Psalm 37:7a*

- **Position yourself often where God can speak to you.** Read the Bible, reflect on Scriptures, and pray for understanding. God has spoken to His people for millennia through His written word; expect Him to speak to you also. Look to Christian preachers, teachers, and authors. Listen to Christian music. Seek God in nature and in the daily tasks of life. Ask God to show you places and times to hear Him. Listen with all your senses, being prayerfully open to ways God will speak to you. Be intentional to set aside times each day to be quiet, to be still and listen for God.

> Whether you turn to the right or to the left, your ears will hear a voice behind you, saying, "This is the way; walk in it." *Isaiah 30:21*

- **Practice persistently.** Listening is a skill that must be developed. Listening to God is a skill He will empower you to develop as you persist in seeking to discern His voice.

For personal reflection and action...

Work on the steps suggested above:

> » Petition God to teach you to listen.
> » Expect to hear God's voice.
> » Position yourself where God can speak and where you are quiet enough to hear.
> » Practice, persist, and do not turn away.
> » Thank God for what He teaches you.

He wakens me morning by morning, wakens my ear to listen like one being instructed. The Sovereign Lord has opened my ears; I have not been rebellious, I have not turned away.
Isaiah 50:4b–5

PRAYER MATTER 14

Don't Fret: Just Pray, and Pray, and Pray

I flagged a devotional some time ago to which I return frequently. The title of the devotional was "Fret Not Thyself," based on Psalm 37:1. That King James lingo seemed just right for this practical advice.

> Therefore do not worry about tomorrow, for tomorrow will worry about itself. Each day has enough trouble of its own. *Matthew 6:34*

> A heart at peace gives life to the body. *Proverbs 14:30*

I often reread that devotional because I have a tendency to worry or, as my grandmother would phrase it, to fret. Once I get on the fretting track, all sorts of things become candidates for worrying. I can worry over family matters, over relationship matters, over matters on my to-do list, or over just about anything.

Common sense tells me that fretting is futile. Most of the things about which I fret do not warrant the time and energy I expend on worrying about them. Many fall into the category of worries about which Mark Train said, "I've had a lot of worries in my life, most of which never happened." Of course,

> Do not be anxious about anything, but in every situation, by prayer and petition, with thanksgiving, present your requests to God. And the peace of God, which transcends all understanding, will guard your hearts and your minds in Christ Jesus. *Philippians 4:6–7*

some things that cause me to fret are very important, and some relate to genuinely hard circumstances. But even in those cases, fretting solves nothing. On the contrary, it saps my energy and clouds my judgment. Worry and fret send me spiraling into negativity, adding worry upon worry.

Jesus says repetitively in Matthew 6, "Do not worry… Can you by worrying add a single hour to your life?… Why do you worry?… So do not worry." Worry robs us of the peace and life God desires for us. Scriptures clearly tell us that God does not want that for His children. And yet, it is hard not to worry. It goes against our worldly nature.

The apostle Paul prescribed the only effective method I have found to combat worry. Knowing our human tendency to fret, he advises us to take our worries to God through prayer. Paul's prescription for fretting is echoed in a poem written in the early 1900s by Edith Willis Linn, "Restless Heart, Don't Worry So."

Dear restless heart, be still! Don't fret and worry so;
God has a thousand ways His love and help to show.
Just trust, and trust, and trust, until His will you know.

Dear restless heart, be still, for peace is God's own smile;
His love can every wrong and sorrow reconcile.
Just love, and love, and love, and calmly wait a while.

Dear restless heart, be brave! Don't moan and sorrow so;
He hath a meaning kind in chilly winds that blow.
Just hope, and hope, and hope, until you braver grow.

Dear restless heart, repose upon His heart an hour;
His heart is strength and life, His love is bloom and
    flower.
Just rest, and rest, and rest, within His tender power.

Dear restless heart, be still! Don't toil and hurry so;
God is the silent One, forever calm and slow;
Just wait, and wait, and wait, and work with Him below.

Dear restless heart, be still! Don't struggle to be free;
God's life is in your life; from Him you may not flee.
Just pray, and pray, and pray, till you have faith to see.

– Edith Willis Linn

The next time you find yourself drawn into the downward spiral of worry and fret, heed the advice of Paul and Edith—"Don't fret. Just pray, and pray, and pray."

A Personal Postscript

You may think, "There are times I need to worry."
I totally get that. Through our son's roller-coaster
cancer battle, I battled worry continually. But
not worrying does *not* mean not caring. It means
trusting God with our deepest concerns day by
day, hour by hour, so we can function and rest in
Him. The next prayer matter addresses trust.

For personal reflection and action...

Focus this month on turning worries into prayers.
» Become aware of times you worry. **Ask** God
   to nudge you as soon as you begin to fret
   about something.
» Immediately take that worry to God. **Ask** for
   God's help, tell God you trust Him, and **ask**
   for His peace.
» Repeat as often as necessary.

PRAYER MATTER 15

Prayer and Trust

> Some trust in chariots and some in horses, but we trust in the name of the Lord our God. *Psalm 20:7*

My church ladies' group once did a Bible study that strongly reinforced the trustworthiness of our Sovereign Lord. Along with the study, we read Scriptures that again and again point us to trust God. We shared instances where God had proven His trustworthiness over and over in our own lives.

It struck us as ironic that often right after a great lesson inspiring us to trust God, we would raise prayer requests in ways that revealed excessive anxiety. We began prompting each other to ask whenever such anxiety surfaced, "Do I trust God, or don't I?" We of

> When I am afraid, I put my trust in You. *Psalm 56:3*

> Surely God is my salvation; I will trust and not be afraid. *Isaiah 12:2*

course prayed over every request, but we also encouraged each other to trust more and worry less.

I totally attest to lyrics from an old hymn written by Louisa Stead in the 1880s, "Jesus, Jesus, how I trust Him! How I've proved Him o'er and o'er." Yet, even after all the times my Lord has proven that I can trust Him, there is still the daily temptation to let dangers, toils, and snares of life generate fear and anxiety.

I deeply identify with the father in Mark 9:24. The desperate man had brought his son, who had suffered violent convulsions since childhood, to Jesus for healing. He begged Jesus, "If you can do anything, take pity on us and help us." Jesus replied, "'If you can'? Everything is possible for one who believes." Immediately the father exclaimed, "I do believe; help me overcome my unbelief!"

> Immediately the boy's father exclaimed, "I do believe; help me overcome my unbelief." *Mark 9:24*

I do trust. Yet I need God to help my lack of trust.

Prayer puts us in a position for God to help us. Prayer connects us with the Holy Spirit, Who empowers us to trust and hope. Like manna for the Hebrews in the wilderness, trust must be garnered daily through prayer.

When practices like those suggested below become daily habits, we will find ourselves seldom

> "Trust grows nowhere so readily and so richly as in the prayer chamber. Its unfolding and development are rapid and wholesome when they are regularly and well kept."
> *E. M. Bounds*

having to ask whether or not we trust God. My daily prayer for myself, and for each of you, is that of Paul in Romans 15:13, "May the God of hope fill you with all joy and peace *as you trust in Him*, so that you may overflow with hope by the power of the Holy Spirit."

For personal reflection and action...

» **Ask** God each morning to enable you, through His Holy Spirit, to trust in Him.

» Read Scriptures about trusting in God. Know them; pray them.

When anxiety starts creeping in, ask yourself, "**Do I trust God, or don't I?**"

» Thank God often for your blessings and for past times He helped you through.

» Praise God that He is trustworthy and sovereign, and pray to grasp the significance.

» When a concern arises, stop, tell it to God, and say, preferably out loud, "I trust You with this, God." Do your best to leave it with God and move on.

» Repeat as often as necessary.

PRAYER MATTER 16

Pray for the USA

My pastor frequently reminds our congregation that our hope as Christians is in the Kingdom of God. Yet, in this world, we reside in "host cultures." We are blessed in the United States to live in a host culture that has been highly favored by God. Currently, however, our host culture faces perilous times.

In 1940, the United Kingdom also faced perilous times as it endured months of relentless bombing

> If My people, who are called by My name, will humble themselves and pray and seek My face and turn from their wicked ways, then I will hear from heaven, and I will forgive their sin and will heal their land.
> *2 Chronicles 7:14*

known as The Blitz. Supported by UK's leaders, a Silent Minute was instigated to call people to pause daily and pray for one minute for peace to prevail. The bells of Big Ben were played on the radio each evening as a signal to begin. The practice has been credited with profound results.

My church recently undertook a similar prayer effort. For a period of four months, we were asked at 8 p.m. each evening to stop whatever we were doing and spend one-minute praying for the USA. We were called not to pray during this minute for a specific political outcome or issue, but to pray for God's mercy and God's favor upon our nation.

> But seek the welfare of the city where I have sent you into exile, and pray to the Lord on its behalf, for in its welfare you will find your welfare.
> *Jeremiah 29:7 (ESV)*

I encourage you to determine a length of time you will commit to pray daily for the USA. Determine the time you

> "Not by might nor by power, but by My Spirit," says the Lord Almighty.
> *Zechariah 4:6b*

will pray each day. Implement a mechanism for reminding yourself. Then, every day at that time, for at least one minute, pray for the USA.

Throughout the Bible, prophets, psalmists, and apostles call God's people to pray for the earthly kingdoms in which they reside and for rulers over those kingdoms. The following Scriptures serve as good models for prayer and reflection:

Deuteronomy 28:1–14	Psalm 67	Jonah 3:5–10
I Kings 8:28–30	Psalm 85	1 Timothy 2:1–3
Psalm 2:1–6, 10–12	Daniel 2:20–23a	Romans 13:1–7

For personal reflection and action...

» Determine the length of time you will commit to pray; I suggest a minimum of one month. Note the dates on your calendar.

» Set the daily time for your one-minute prayer. 8 p.m. worked well for our congregation and has been used in other group prayer initiatives. Set your phone or bedside alarm as a daily reminder to stop and pray.

» Consider enlisting a prayer partner or inviting a larger group to join you in praying for this period of time.

» Pray daily.

» Then keep your eyes open for ways God moves, including ways God changes your perspective and heart.

A Personal Postscript

In 2012, I received an e-mail invitation to join an initiative to pray for our nation at 8 p.m. each day. I immediately set my phone reminder. That evening while walking outside the hospital where I was staying with my son, my alarm rang and caught me off guard. The displayed message, "2 Chron PRAY," was a welcome surprise. Pausing immediately to pray, I not only sensed the power of many prayers simultaneously lifted with mine, but I felt a connection with other Christians that lifted me above my personal fears and heartache.

Prayer Matter 17

Then, Why?

Does God answer prayer? I believe with all my heart that He does.

Then, why_____? Most of us who have lived very long can fill in our own blank.

When life seems unfair. When we know God has power to do all things. When what we prayed for seemed so in accordance with God's will... *Then, why?*

I have asked my own *Then, why?* questions, especially when our son David died after hundreds of people had prayed with great faith that he would be healed on this earth. With my heart breaking, I have in such times asked God, "Then, why?"

I am often led back to the book of Job, the Bible's treatise on the mystery of human suffering. Like Job, I have taken my questions to God. Like Job, I also have learned not to presume that the Almighty God, Who laid the earth's foundation, is obliged to answer. And yet, God has always graciously responded—not necessarily with an answer, but with insight, reassurance, and comfort.

In addition, in the shadow of my seemingly unanswered "huge" prayers, God has revealed many "small" answered prayers. As I look back on the hardest of times in my life, I am now able to discern God's grace and mercy in many circumstances, which I could not see at the time. The sum of these small answered prayers is astounding in retrospect.

Then Job replied to the Lord:

"I know that You can do all things; no purpose of Yours can be thwarted. You asked, 'Who is this that obscures my plans without knowledge?' Surely I spoke of things I did not understand, things too wonderful for me to know.

You said, 'Listen now, and I will speak; I will question you, and you shall answer me.' My ears had heard of You but now my eyes have seen You.

Therefore I despise myself and repent in dust and ashes." *Job 42:1–6*

May the God of hope fill you with all joy and peace as you trust in Him, so that you may overflow with hope by the power of the Holy Spirit. *Romans 15:13*

When you have your own *Then, why?* questions, take them directly to God. Ask Him to make you receptive to His instruction and comfort.

In accordance with Romans 15:13, God will provide hope through the darkest of times. In accordance with Romans 8:28, He will work in all things for the good of those who love Him, though we may not see it now.

In accordance with 2 Corinthians 12:9, His grace will meantime suffice.

Someday, we will fully understand all of life's *Then why's?* Until then, according to 2 Corinthians 5:7, we just keep walking with God, one step at a time, by faith and not by sight.

> And we know that in all things God works for the good of those who love Him, who have been called according to His purpose. *Romans 8:28*

> But He said to me, "My grace is sufficient for you, for My power is made perfect in weakness." Therefore I will boast all the more gladly about my weaknesses, so that Christ's power may rest on me. *2 Corinthians 12:9*

> For we live by faith, not by sight. *2 Corinthians 5:7*

For personal reflection and action...

» When you have *Then, why?* questions, take them to God.

» Be honest. Tell God what you are feeling—whether hurt or perplexed or angry. Our all-knowing God knows already how you feel. **Ask** God to help you.

> Sometimes, it may be all you can do to pray, "God I am hurting. I do not understand. Please help me." At those times, that is enough.

» Prepare yourself in advance to weather life's storms. Familiarize yourself with God's promises. Reflect on God's character. **Ask** God to grow your faith.

PRAYER MATTER 18

Prayers God Delights to Answer "Yes"

The last prayer matter acknowledged that we sometimes have *Then, why?* questions about prayers that are not answered according to our personal expectations. Such questions may be fueled by Scriptures that seem to promise that God will answer whatever we ask in faith.

> "So I say to you: Ask and it will be given to you; seek and you will find; knock and the door will be opened to you." *Luke 11:9*

While wrestling with the profound mystery of prayer, I have come to believe there are indeed many prayers that God delights always to answer, but such prayers do not encompass "whatever." For example, in Luke 11:9,

> "If you remain in me and my words remain in you, ask whatever you wish, and it will be done for you." *John 15:7*

Jesus said "Ask and it will be given to you," and then verse 13 clarifies that the asking is for the Holy Spirit. In John 15:7, "ask whatever you wish" is linked in the next verse to bearing fruit to God's glory.

Bottom line, I believe prayers that God always answers *Yes* are those that reflect the desire to grow closer to God and become more like Christ. *Yes* prayers do not expect guaranteed answers for specific earthly outcomes, but rather acknowledge God's sovereign will and seek strength to trust and obey God whatever the outcome. They do not attempt to change God, but rather ask that God change me—my heart, my attitude, and my perspective.

Don't get me wrong; I often pray very specific intercessory prayers. I believe with all my heart that God hears and works through such prayers—often with miraculous demonstrations. However, it has been my experience that those are not the guaranteed *Yes* prayers.

Example "Yes" Prayers

Lord…

- Fill me with Your Spirit.
- Forgive me.
- Use me; let me bear fruit to Your glory.
- Help me love You (and others) more.
- Increase my faith through this trial.
- Have mercy.
- Give me hope.
- Teach me what You want me to know.
- Help me be a light in this dark world.
- Show me Your presence.

Perhaps as I continue to grow in Christ and learn better to pray in the Spirit, my fervent prayers for God's specific intercession will become more aligned with God's will and thus with the promise that whatever I ask in Jesus' name will be done.

But I suspect I will continue to struggle this side of Heaven with the how's and why's of prayer. Thus, even as I continue to pray fervently and persistently as best I can for

> For no matter how many promises God has made, they are "Yes" in Christ.
> 2 *Corinthians 1:20a*

those I hold dear, I have resolved to trust and obey God whatever the outcomes. I am also resolving to be more intent, and to pray more often, those prayers God promises to answer with *Yes*. I can't wait to see how God changes me!

A Personal Postscript

Until his last breath, I never stopped fervently praying and believing in faith that God would heal my son on earth. As David declined in his last days, I began also to pray that whatever happened, God would continue to give our family hope—even amidst the horrific grief I knew would befall us if David should die. God put a Scripture in my heart; I prayed it over and over, and still do. My prayer for David's earthly healing was not answered, but God said *Yes* to my Romans 15:13 prayer. Mingled with our tears, we have experienced hope and peace beyond human possibility.

For personal reflection and action...

» Choose one of these *Yes* prayers, or one of your own. Focus on praying it daily.
» Find and read Scriptures that speak to your prayer focus. For instance, if you are praying for peace, reflect on Scriptures such as Psalm 4:8, Isaiah 26:3, John 14:27, and Philippians 4:4–7.
» Watch expectantly for ways God will answer your prayer.
» Be sure to thank God for answering!

PRAYER MATTER 19

The Lord's Prayer

When Jesus' disciples asked him, "Lord, teach us to pray," Jesus responded by teaching them the prayer that we know as the Lord's Prayer. The Lord's Prayer has become the most well-known prayer among both Christians and non-Christians alike.

> One day Jesus was praying in a certain place. When he finished, one of his disciples said to him, "Lord, teach us to pray, just as John taught his disciples." He said to them, "When you pray, say: 'Father, hallowed be Your name, Your kingdom come...'" *Luke 11:1–2*

Most of us know and have often prayed this prayer. My congregation prays the Lord's Prayer aloud as we worship together weekly. Praying it frequently is both powerful and comforting.

Yet, sometimes, familiarity can mask the depth, richness, and complexity of this brief prayer. It the best model for prayer that we have, because it shows us how Jesus prayed.

Our Father in heaven,

> Jesus invites us to come before God as children approaching a perfect, loving father, except this Father is our Almighty God, Who reigns in Heaven.

Hallowed be Thy name.

> The first petition, that God's name be hallowed, is both a reverent expression of praise for God's holy character and a fervent prayer that God's name be hallowed by all.

Thy kingdom come, Thy will be done, on earth as it is in heaven.

> We pray for the ultimate establishment of God's rule; we long for Heaven. We also pray that His will be done here and now, on Earth. This positions us to desire that our will be aligned with what God wants.

Give us this day our daily bread,

> We are now positioned to pray for our daily necessities, both physical and spiritual.

And forgive us our debts as we forgive our debtors.

> Even as we are told to ask forgiveness for our sins, we are also instructed to forgive others. Pray for grace to forgive, and for the release and peace that come from forgiving.

And lead us not into temptation, but deliver us from evil.

> We know we are not strong enough on our own to resist those forces that tempt us to disobey God. So we pray that in His grace, God will steer us away from sin and evil.

The Lord's Prayer is one of Jesus' teachings that we should know by heart. If we pray this prayer as it is, really thinking about the meaning of each phrase and asking God to touch and teach us in fresh ways as we pray it, it is life changing. Praying the Lord's Prayer from memory is also powerful at times when we are otherwise at a loss for words.

But beyond praying the exact words, Jesus also gave us a pattern and principles for praying. He approached God as his Father, which was previously unheard of. He focused first on God's Holy character and then prayed to align his will with the Father's. Only then did Jesus turn to personal requests—for provision, forgiveness, and God's guidance and protection in a world wrought with temptation and evil.

Focus on the Lord's Prayer in the weeks ahead. Thank God for this example, and ask Him to touch and teach you in fresh ways as you pray the prayer Jesus taught us.

For personal reflection and action…

» Meditate on each element encompassed in the Lord's Prayer.

» Pray the Lord's Prayer daily for the next weeks. Pray it as it is, or rephrase in your own words, in light of your current circumstances.

» Try substituting "me" for "our" as you pray in private.

» When you pray the Lord's Prayer with others, do so with renewed focus and fervor.

PRAYER MATTER 20

Bless This House

House is defined as the place where someone lives. Home is almost synonymous, perhaps with a more permanent connotation. Either way, our houses are very

> By wisdom a house is built, and through understanding it is established; through knowledge its rooms are filled with rare and beautiful treasures.
> *Proverbs 24:3–4*

significant places. As the backdrop for key events in our lives, homes have power to color those events and thus our memories in positive or negative ways.

I remember every house in which Mike and I have lived since our marriage—from our first little apartment, to a tiny duplex, to a series of small rent houses, to the three houses we have owned. We went through

> My people will live in peaceful dwelling places, in secure homes, in undisturbed places of rest.
> *Isaiah 32:18*

many of the ups and downs of life while we lived in each house, but even in the bad times, I always considered our home as a haven of rest and security. I attribute the positive aura of each house to the routine practice I had learned of praying God's blessing upon each one.

Blessing one's home is a wonderful idea. If we believe in the power of prayer, certainly it makes sense to ask for God's favor and protection over the space where we spend so much of our lives with those we love.

It is also a wonderful idea to bless the home of another. When sending followers out to do his work, Jesus told them to pronounce peace upon every house they entered. When I have been in a home where our pastor has been present, he has offered a prayer of blessing over the host's home. A blessing is a meaningful gift we can give to others, under our authority as followers of Jesus Christ.

> "When you enter a house, first say, 'Peace to this house.'" *Luke 10:5*

Make it a point this month to bless, or re-bless, your home. Be open to opportunities to say, "Peace to this house," when entering the home of another. By asking God to take authority over our homes, we are inviting Him into our lives. Like Joshua, we are voicing that we

> "As for me and my house, we will serve the Lord." *Joshua 24:15b*

choose to serve the Lord. By entrusting our homes to Him, we claim God's peace and love for all who dwell within.

A Personal Postscript

I recently helped my daughter's family settle in their new home. While all were away, I walked through to bless each room. In the kitchen I prayed for love and bonding over meals to be shared over the years; in the living and family rooms, I prayed for blessed interactions with family and friends. I prayed especially in the bedrooms for rest, protection, and God's sensed presence. I prayed God's Spirit would fill every space so mightily that whoever enters will tangibly sense welcome, peace, and safety.

I will soon get to pray over a home that my daughter-in-law is buying. But meantime I often walk by and pray from the outside for God's protection and blessing. I also pray through the neighborhood for safety, welcoming neighbors, and a godly environment.

It comforts me greatly to entrust these I love so much into God's daily keeping.

For personal reflection and action…

» Pray your own simple prayer to bless your home. I pray for God's Spirit to fill every room with God's protection, peace, and love. I pray all who enter the home will sense that this is a safe place, where they are welcome. Often I walk through the house and pray over various rooms, specifically asking for God's blessing on the activities and people associated with that space. I like to touch the walls as I do so.

» Frame a poem or Scripture blessing, and hang it in your home as a visual reminder that you entrust your home to God.

» Pray over homes of friends and loved ones— either privately or aloud as appropriate.

Prayer Matter 21

Be Like Aaron and Hur

Soon after Moses led his people out of Egypt into the wilderness, they fought their first battle. While they were encamped at Rephadim, the Israelites were attacked by the Amalekites.

Read Exodus 17:8–16 for a full account of the battle.

Moses sent Joshua out to fight, while Moses himself stood on top of the hill and held up the staff of God. As long as Moses held up the staff, the Israelites were winning the battle, but

> So Joshua fought the Amalekites as Moses had ordered, and Moses, Aaron and Hur went to the top of the hill. As long as Moses held up his hands, the Israelites were winning, but whenever he lowered his hands, the Amalekites were winning. When Moses' hands grew tired, they took a stone and put it under him and he sat on it. Aaron and Hur held his hands up—one on one side, one on the other—so that his hands remained steady till sunset. So Joshua overcame the Amalekite army with the sword. *Exodus 17:10–13*

when he lowered his hands, the Amalekites were winning. When Moses became tired, Aaron and Hur stepped in to support Moses in raising his hands. Moses was thus able to hold up the staff all day, so Joshua could defeat the enemy.

This account provides a compelling picture of God's Kingdom, where battles are won through obedience in both action and prayer. Sometimes believers are called to be like Joshua and take courageous action on the field. Other times, we are called to be like Moses and stand on the hill, providing primary and active support for those on the front lines. Yet other times, we are called to be like Aaron and Hur, serving on the sidelines to lift faithfully in prayer those on the fore-front so they do not tire.

Through different seasons and circumstances, believers are called by God to assume varying roles. There is always a role for everyone, even if there are seasons when all we can do is lift our hands in prayer. And when we have the benefit of looking back from Heaven upon our earthly accomplishments, we just may discover that those "all we can do" times were the most effective seasons of our lives.

A Personal Postscript

Our son underwent two stem-cell transplants in a Dallas hospital, where I spent many weeks living with him. Away from home, fearing for David's life, I prayed constantly for him. But God also put it on my heart to pray for friends and church family back home who were enduring physical, emotional, and financial trials, as well as for our church leaders and programs. Temporarily sidelined from direct duties, I continually lifted others in prayer. Doing so kept me from fixating on our heartache and provided an uplifting connection with others. I believe it also impacted the lives of those for whom I prayed in ways I will never know this side of Heaven. I am convinced that in Heaven we will have the joy of finally knowing the immense power of prayer.

For personal reflection and action...

» **Ask** God each morning who needs your prayers this day. Imitate Aaron and Hur by praying alongside those whose hands and hearts need lifting.

» **Ask** God to give you a heart to pray for others.

> For now we see indistinctly, as in a mirror, but then face to face. Now I know in part, but then I will know fully, as I am fully known.
> *1 Corinthians 13:12 (HCSB)*

» **Ask** Him to give you faith to believe that prayer works, even when you do not see direct results.

» **Ask** God, in His grace, to give you enough sight occasionally to see the impact of prayer, and watch for ways God answers. Praise Him that one day we will fully see the impact!

» If you are unable to serve in direct ways during this season of your life, take heart! Take on the ministry of prayer, and trust that your service is consecrated and highly effective.

Prayer Matter 22

Prayer Bowls

I recently received a very special Christmas gift—a prayer bowl, which is designed as a repository for prayer requests. On the rim of the bowl is inscribed Philippians 4:6, which is one of my favorite Scriptures. Instead of being anxious, the apostle Paul admonishes us to take

> Do not be anxious about anything, but in prayer and petition, with thanksgiving, present your requests to God. *Philippians 4:6*

our requests directly to God in prayer and petition.

The rationale for the bowl is that we hear daily of many prayer requests, through friends, church, news, social media, etc. While we genuinely intend to pray for many of these needs, too often they get lost as we proceed with our daily routines. The idea is, instead, to pause long enough to print off or jot down each request for which we intend to pray, and place the slip of paper in the prayer bowl. Keep the prayer bowl somewhere you spend time daily. At some point—preferably a consistent time—go through the slips and lift up the requests in prayer to God.

Visual reminders are great prayer prompts. Indeed, in the busyness of life, we often forget to pray even those concerns that are closest to our hearts. Lists and sticky notes are examples of pen-and-paper visuals, which I have used—on my bathroom mirror, on my computer, in my car, etc. Nowadays, electronic reminders abound, including prayer prompter apps for smartphones. These are especially great for those who are more tuned in to technology.

> Rejoice always; pray continually…
> *1 Thessalonians 5:16–17*

> And pray in the Spirit on all occasions with all kinds of prayers and requests. With this in mind, be alert and always keep on praying for all the Lord's people. *Ephesians 6:18*

The prayer bowl is another option, which I have come to treasure. One reason the bowl is special is that it reminds me of the special friends who gave it to me. But it also reminds me of a verse in Revelation that describes, before God's Heavenly throne, golden bowls full of incense—the prayers of God's people. That is not only a beautiful picture, but it is also a powerful confirmation that our prayers truly matter, even extending to Heaven. And it is yet another confirmation that, when we get to Heaven, we will see the

> … and they were holding golden bowls full of incense, which are the prayers of God's people. *Revelation 5:8b*

difference all our prayers have made in the lives of our loved ones and in God's Kingdom.

For personal reflection and action...

» Create your own prayer bowl by purchasing or using a bowl, basket, or other container for holding your written prayer requests. It can be as simple or as decorative as you wish.

» Follow the instructions quoted above, or personalize your own method for using your prayer bowl. I keep my prayer bowl in my prayer closet/nook, and then draw out written slips and pray over a few at a time. Two of our friends, a married couple, keep their prayer bowl beside their bed; they draw requests each night, kneel beside the bed, and pray together before bedtime.

» Sometimes I write just a name, and sometimes I write a brief summary of the request. Some requests are long-term; some cover shorter-term situations. Although we will not know how God acts upon all the prayers in our earthly bowls, for many we will see wonderful outcomes. Whenever I retire a request from my bowl, I thank God for hearing the prayer, praise Him for specific results, and entrust to Him those still "pending."

PRAYER MATTER 23

Wield Your Shield of Faith

Ephesians 6:10–18 tells us how to be strong in the Lord and in His mighty power by putting on the full armor of God. Please take a few minutes to read the whole Scripture.

Recently, Mike and I experienced a series of "domestic trials." A home remodel was repeatedly extended and displaced us for weeks. Meanwhile, our sewer line collapsed and led to a sewer nightmare, with one issue after another.

> Finally, be strong in the Lord and in His mighty power. Put on the full armor of God, so that you can take your stand against the devil's schemes… In addition to all this, take up the shield of faith, with which you can extinguish all the flaming arrows of the evil one. *Ephesians 6:10–11, 16*

Then, unrelated plumbing problems brought additional damage and expense.

Weeks of nonstop problems became physically and mentally trying. After a while, to prevent their robbing me of peace, I began to think of each setback as a flaming arrow and envisioned deflecting it with the shield of faith. Although it helped, I chided myself that these were mere irritations in the scheme of life, and I decided that I should save my shield of faith for true tribulations.

The very next time I prayed, however, it came to me that warriors do not employ their weapons for the first time in a major battle. Rather, they train continually in non-life-and-death situations, over and over, until use of the weapons becomes second nature.

> The weapons we fight with are not the weapons of the world. On the contrary, they have divine power to demolish strongholds.
> *2 Corinthians 10:4*

I discerned that it *is* most appropriate to practice wielding the shield of faith, as well as other spiritual weapons, as often as possible. Not only does such practice prepare us to battle genuine tribulations, but it also deflects those irritations that may be minor in the big picture of life but nevertheless have power daily to rob our peace and lessen our witness.

So, I encourage you to practice wielding your shield over these next weeks. Whatever trials come at you each day, whether minor irritations or major tribulations, pray and picture yourself deflecting each as you hold up the shield that represents your faith. In the name of Jesus, ask God for His power, protection, and peace.

For personal reflection and action...

» Practice wielding your shield of faith. Whenever a trial comes your way, imagine deflecting it with your shield held firmly in place (I literally hold up my forearm as if deflecting the attack), while praying that God would extinguish

> Therefore put on the full armor of God, so that when the day of evil comes, you may be able to stand your ground, and after you have done everything, to stand. *Ephesians 6:13*

that flaming arrow, restore mental peace, and give you discernment and strength to deal with it appropriately through the power of the Holy Spirit.

» To intercede for someone else, imagine holding a shield above that person as you pray that all arrows bombarding your loved one be deflected.

» The shield of faith is only one part of the "full armor of God." Read Ephesians 6:10–18 often; preferably, memorize this powerful Scripture. Become well acquainted with all parts of God's armor, which include the belt of truth, breastplate of righteousness, readiness that comes from the gospel of peace, shield of faith, helmet of salvation, sword of the Spirit, and prayer. Then, make it your practice daily to gear up in full armor!

PRAYER MATTER 24

Ask!

Asking comes more naturally to some people than to others. I am one for whom asking has always felt awkward. Partly, I don't want to bother people. Partly, I would prefer handling things myself. Partly, I have a streak of shyness. This reluctance to ask has carried over into my prayer life. While I am quite bold to intercede on behalf of others, I have seldom asked anything for myself.

> "Whether we like it or not, asking is the rule of the Kingdom."
> *C. H. Spurgeon*

God recently opened my eyes to the importance of asking, as I read Scripture after Scripture clearly declaring that God wants us to ask, not only for others, but also for God's gifts for ourselves.

Luke 11:1–13 combines key teachings of Jesus about prayer. After model-

> "So I say to you, Ask and it will be given to you; seek and you will find; knock and the door will be opened to you."
> *Luke 11:9*

ing for his disciples the Lord's Prayer, Jesus told a parable of a friend asking for bread at midnight. The parable of this persistent friend led into Jesus' teaching to **ask**, **s**eek, and **k**nock (**ask**). Then Jesus posed a question any loving parent would understand: If your child asks for a fish, will you give him a snake? It is an outrageous thought, but the point is clear: how much more does God, in His absolute goodness, delight to give good gifts to those who ask Him.

> Until now you have not asked for anything in my name. Ask and you will receive, and your joy will be complete. *John 16:24*

> "If you then, though you are evil, know how to give good gifts to your children, how much more will your Father in heaven give the Holy Spirit to those who ask Him!" *Luke 11:13*

Part of the confusion related to this asking is that sometimes we interpret Scriptures about asking to mean we can ask for anything we want and get it, if we pray hard. Thus, when we pray for such "anythings" and fail to receive them, we may become discouraged.

In light of my expanded perspective on asking, I did a novel thing—I **asked**

> If any of you lacks wisdom, you should ask God, who gives generously to all without finding fault, and it will be given to you. *James 1:5*

God to help me understand. I have since noticed the kinds of good gifts specified in Scriptures about asking. These good gifts include the Holy Spirit, living water, joy, wisdom, knowledge of God's will, and other spiritual gifts. Like children, we can ask God for anything on our hearts, but when asking for such spiritual gifts, we can approach God with the utmost assurance that He will give us good gifts.

James put it perhaps most succinctly: "You do not have because you do not ask" *(James 4:2b)*. That is a mistake I intend to avoid in the future, now that I have learned "the rule of the Kingdom."

A Personal Postscript

My granddaughter is not the least bit shy about asking. Whether school fundraising, seeking information, wanting something, or just curious—she simply and outright asks. Not only is she bold to ask, but negative responses have not deterred her continuing to ask. I am trying to learn from her!

For personal reflection and action…

» Read and reflect on Jesus' teachings on prayer in Luke 11:1–13, as well as the other Scriptures referenced. **Ask** God to lead you to other Scriptures and writings about the importance of asking God for good gifts.

» **Ask** your Heavenly Father to increase your boldness in asking Him for good gifts. Pray daily for the Holy Spirit to bring to mind those spiritual gifts you most need that day and to nudge you to pray for them.

» **Ask** for persistence in asking. In the words of one Bible translation, "And so it is with prayer—keep on asking and you will keep on getting" *Luke 11:9a (TLB).*

Prayer Matter 25

Father, Forgive

We are bombarded by news of intense suffering in the world. While some suffering results from natural circumstances, most suffering results from human evil, hatred, greed, pride, and indifference. Such news can drive us to deep discouragement.

The first thing to do with such discouragement is to take it to God. I did so recently and was reminded of a trip I took with our church choir in 1994 to Coventry Cathedral in England. It was a memorable trip. What I remember most is the remarkable blend of old and new, with the modern 20th century cathedral standing in sharp contrast to the ruined shell of its medieval predecessor.

You see, in 1940, the cathedral was bombed and destroyed. The Provost, walking through the charred ruins, took three medieval nails from the smoldering roof timbers and wired them together in the shape of a cross. He determined that, in witness to the resurrection of Jesus Christ after death on the cross, the cathedral would become a symbol of grace and forgiveness, and with God's blessing, would ultimately "rise again."

Coventry Litany of Reconciliation

All have sinned and fallen short of the glory of God.

The hatred which divides nation from nation, race from race, class from class,
　　Father, forgive.
The covetous desires of people and nations to possess what is not their own,
　　Father, forgive.
The greed which exploits the work of human hands and lays waste the earth,
　　Father, forgive.
Our envy of the welfare and happiness of others,
　　Father, forgive.
Our indifference to the plight of the imprisoned, the homeless, the refugee,
　　Father, forgive.
The lust which dishonors the bodies of men, women and children,
　　Father, forgive.
The pride which leads us to trust in ourselves and not in God,
　　Father, forgive.

Be kind to one another, tender-hearted, forgiving one another, as God in Christ forgave you.

Source: Coventry Cathedral, Coventry England – Reprinted with permission.

That cross of nails became the inspiration for a mission of reconciliation, which—as opposed to lamenting or hating—worked to help people around the world live in peace, including their German foes. The ministry and the new Coventry Cathedral, consecrated in 1962, stand today as testaments to reconciliation.

In my recent quiet time, I recalled standing in the ruins of the old cathedral and reading the words, "Father, Forgive" inscribed on the wall. I was reminded that, instead of focusing on bad, evil, or hatred, I can make the conscious choice to love and reach out. That is not the easy or natural choice. The only way I can come close is to ask for God's help in loving my enemies, which Jesus has commanded His followers to do. I can ask God to change my heart, so that I see every person through the eyes of Jesus, who asked God to forgive even those who crucified him. And I can remember that I am a person just as much in need of forgiveness as those who crucified Jesus.

> Jesus said, "Father, forgive them, for they do not know what they are doing." *Luke 23:34a*

> But I tell you, love your enemies and pray for those who persecute you. *Matthew 5:44*

For personal reflection and action...

» Focus this week on **asking** God to help you love your enemies.

» Reflect on your own need for God's forgiveness.

» **Ask** God to help you be kinder and more tender-hearted toward others, forgiving others as God in Christ forgave you. **Ask** God to show you how you can follow through with action in reaching out.

» Reflect on, and pray through, the Covenant Litany of Reconciliation regularly. Because its points so directly relate to many of the world's distressing problems, the litany is a good prayer to pray whenever these issues loom at the forefront of current news.

PRAYER MATTER 26

The Best Way to Pray

What is the best way to pray? You are halfway through these prayer matters. Although several suggestions have been offered for prayer, they do not begin to scratch the surface of possibilities. You can pray kneeling, bowing, standing, sitting, etc. You can pray in your prayer closet, at your table or desk, in bed, outside, in the car or on the subway, in church, etc. You can pray prayers of intercession or confession. You can ask through prayers of supplication, or you can worship through prayers of adoration. You can pray Scriptures, hymns, or model prayers, such as the Lord's Prayer or the Prayer of St. Francis. Possible types, techniques, and tools for prayer are unending.

> Now this is eternal life: that they know You, the only true God, and Jesus Christ, whom You have sent. *John 17:3*

What is the best way to pray?

Let's start with the supposition that the true goal of prayer is to walk more closely with God, to know Him more personally. The more personally we know God, the more we want to be in His presence, the more we trust Him, and the more we want to become like Him through imitating God's Son, Jesus Christ.

Think of someone to whom you are closest in a positive relationship—someone you know the best, and who knows you the best. Perhaps it is a spouse, relative, or friend. How did you come to know that person intimately? It was not likely one way, but rather through many ways of interacting and communicating over time. Intimacy evolves through talking and listening, through sharing experiences, through laughing and crying together, through learning to trust, and often through trial and error.

> Draw near to God, and He will draw near to you. *James 4:8a*

The same is true of prayer. There is not a single "best way" to pray. What matters is that you do pray, and persist in praying, with the desire to grow in your prayer life and your relationship with your Heavenly Father.

So, try different ways. The best way to pray is whatever draws you to pray. The best way to pray is whatever helps you walk more closely with God in each specific situation or season.

Take confidence in the assurance that prayer is not a one-way street. God's desire that you walk more closely with Him exceedingly outweighs your own. God wants you to draw near to Him. You

> I sought the Lord and He heard me, and delivered me from all my fears. *Psalm 34:4*

can rest assured that whenever and however you pray, your Heavenly Father is waiting to meet you way more than halfway.

> God met me more than halfway; He freed me from my anxious fears. *Psalm 34:4 (MSG)*

For personal reflection and action…

» Try different techniques and tools.
» Strive for balance. One way is to include ACTS: **A**doration, **C**onfession, **T**hanksgiving, and **S**upplication.
» Learn to be still in God's presence and listen.
» Strive to be ever more open and honest. As our pastor says, "Give God your heart."
» Pray always that God will bring your will more and more into alignment with His. Pray to become ever more Christlike.
» Pray to pray. (Refer to Prayer Matter 10.)
» Always remember, God will meet you more than halfway.

PRAYER MATTER 27

Saying Grace

As a child, my most frequent exposure to prayer was through blessings over meals. Although I grew up in a Christian family, prayers were mostly private. Except in times of crisis, I do not recall my parents praying with me over day-to-day concerns. I knew prayer was important and that my parents prayed privately, but I really didn't know how or how often. I do, however, vividly remember my family praying together before meals as a regular practice in our home or at extended family gatherings.

> And when he had said these things, he took bread, and giving thanks to God in the presence of all he broke it and began to eat. *Acts 27:35 (NKJV)*

I have come to realize what a special gift that was. I have also come to recognize the immense value of regular mealtime prayers—or, as my grandparents called it, "saying grace." The practice is important for multiple reasons, which include the following:

- It provides a prayer connection with God two or three times daily. Once established, the habit becomes second nature. I sometimes realize in the midst of a crazy week that I have neglected daily quiet time, but my husband and I never forget to say grace before each meal.

- It is a simple way to learn and practice prayer. Taking my turn saying grace was how I first learned to pray aloud in front of others. It was not threatening, since mealtime prayers are usually "short and sweet." I probably started out with, "God is great, God is good. Let us thank Him for our food." Or I repeated a version of the prayer my Daddy often said, "Bless this food to the nourishment of our bodies, and bless us to Your service." Over time, it became natural to express my own words of blessing. Thus, long before I was comfortable praying a general prayer in public, I could readily pronounce a blessing before a meal—all because of our regular family practice.

- Saying grace is a natural, unassuming way of witnessing to others our belief in God and our Lord Jesus Christ. Over the years we have shared meals in our home with believers who do not regularly pray, for whom the brief blessing may provide a simple, non-threatening example of prayer. We have also shared meals with nonbelievers, for whom the blessing may provide a needed connection to God.

- Most important, saying grace acknowledges God as the source of our food and, indeed, of all our blessings. Saying grace reminds us over and over, in a culture where acquisition and self-sufficiency are paramount, that God is our Provider. When expressed with heartfelt thanksgiving, it is an excellent way of expressing gratitude to our Heavenly Father.

A Personal Postscript

My father experienced Alzheimer's during his last years, and sadly, there came a time when this most intelligent man could barely put a coherent sentence together. Even then, when asked by an aide to bless the meal for residents at his care facility, Roy stood and pronounced as beautiful and full a blessing as ever. On many occasions after he lost basic ability to communicate, Daddy could still say grace—a lifetime habit whose brain connections God still enabled to click.

For personal reflection and action...

» Be intentional to develop and practice the habit of saying grace before every meal. Pray with whomever is present. If you are alone, use your voice and pray out loud.

» Consider expanding mealtime prayers. Since we already have this designated prayer time, Mike and I regularly expand our meal blessing to cover other prayer concerns on our hearts.

» Use meal blessings as opportunities to model and teach prayer with children and grandchildren. Encourage them to take turns offering grace. Be prepared to smile at their creative expressions of thanks, which may often be "outside the box."

» Develop the habit of praying in restaurants. Although this may feel a bit awkward at first, I have come to believe that holding hands and unobtrusively saying grace in public both glorifies God and serves as a quiet witness to others.

» **Ask** God to remind you to say grace and to show you new ways to expand the practice.

PRAYER MATTER 28

Prayer vs. Fear

In many Scriptures, we are clearly told not to fear. Knowing these Scriptures, a friend shared that often she feels disobedient. She often experiences fear. I told her, "Me, too."

I view fear as a natural response to a perceived threat. When ambushed by imminent danger or devastating news, my gut instinctively clinches in fear. But I don't view that initial reaction as disobedient or lacking in faith, just human. It is the next steps that measure faith and obedience. When my mind catches up with my gut, I can yield to fear or I can turn to God.

When I pray, "God, I am afraid. Please help

> Do not be afraid; do not be discouraged, for the Lord your God will be with you wherever you go. *Joshua 1:9b*

> You will not fear the terror of night, nor the arrow that flies by day, nor the pestilence that stalks in the darkness, nor the plague that destroys at midday. *Psalm 91:5–6*

me," I picture Him as a loving parent. Knowing how touched I am when a scared child runs to me, I imagine God experiencing that same tender love, and I trust He will respond. And not only will He respond in the crisis, but He will also invite me to stay close to Him so He can calm my lingering, perpetual fears and be right there with me through every ensuing crisis.

> So do not fear, for I am with you; do not be dismayed, for I am your God. I will strengthen you and help you; I will uphold you with My righteous right hand. *Isaiah 41:10*

We each must choose. We can live in a state of fear; certainly we live in a world where there is much legitimately to fear. We can scurry to God in prayer every time fear becomes overwhelming. Or, we can develop an

> The angel said to them, "Do not be afraid. I bring you good news that will cause great joy for all the people. Today in the town of David a Savior has been born to you; He is the Messiah, the Lord." *Luke 2:10–11*

> "Do not let your hearts be troubled and do not be afraid." *John 14:27b*

ever-deepening relationship with our Heavenly Father and remain close to Him through continual prayer.

The third option will take intentional effort and discipline. But it will yield great joy, as we live more and more in light of the good news of Christ, our Savior, rather than the fearful news of this world. I invite you to join me in putting forth that effort. For only then will we be able confidently to proclaim with the psalmist, "The Lord is my light and my salvation; whom shall I fear? The Lord is the strength of my life; of whom shall I be afraid?" (*Psalm 27:1*).

> For God has not given us a spirit of fear, but of power and of love and of a sound mind. *2 Timothy 1:7 (NKJV)*

For personal reflection and action...

» The next time you are ambushed by a fearful situation, or if you just find fear and anxiety creeping up on you through daily challenges or disheartening media reports, stop to pray. Tell God you are afraid and **ask** Him to help you.

» Create your own list of Scriptures or quotes that call on God to combat your fear. I have clung to the ones shown, but there are many more. Choose your favorites and memorize them, or keep a copy close to you. Quote them to yourself often. Ask God to help you internalize and take them to heart.

» Resolve to live according to the third option described above. Knowing that many of life's worst crises befall us suddenly and without warning, ask God each day to grant you the spirit of power, love, and a sound mind advocated in 2 Timothy 1:7. Pray often, stay close to your Heavenly Father, and continually preach to yourself the truth of God's calming power and presence.

PRAYER MATTER 29

Does Prayer Change God's Mind?

There are instances in the Bible where God pronounced judgment and then seems to have been persuaded to relent.

> "There is no power like that of prevailing prayer, of Abraham pleading for Sodom, Jacob wrestling in the stillness of the night, Moses standing in the breach, Hannah intoxicated with sorrow, David heartbroken with remorse and grief, Jesus in sweat of blood. Add to this list from the records of the church your personal observation and experience, and always there is the cost of passion unto blood. Such prayer prevails. It turns ordinary mortals into men of power. It brings power. It brings fire. It brings rain. It brings life. It brings God. "
> *Samuel Chadwick*

In one account, Abraham pled with God not to destroy Sodom (*Genesis 18:20–33*). After God had declared His intent to destroy the wicked city, Abraham negotiated with

God to spare Sodom if fifty righteous people could be found. When God agreed, Abraham continued to negotiate the number down until God answered, "For the sake of ten, I will not destroy it."

In another account, Moses pled with God not to destroy the Israelites in God's anger after they made an idol shaped like a golden calf (*Exodus 32:9–14*). Moses delivered an impassioned case and called on God's promises. "Then, the Lord relented and did not bring on His people the disaster He had threatened."

I used to wonder how an unchanging God could seemingly be persuaded to change His mind in such instances. Then it occurred to me that God was teaching Abraham and Moses, as well as you and me, to intercede on behalf of others. Rather than wonder, now I am simply grateful and amazed that our all-knowing God would be so gracious as to accept our input. God is Sovereign. He does not need us, but He chooses to listen and respond to the prayers of His people.

> "Prayer does not influence God. Prayer surely does influence God. It does not influence His purpose. It does influence His action." *S.D. Gordon*

> I urge, then, first of all, that petitions, prayers, intercession and thanksgiving be made for all people. *1 Timothy 2:1*

> And pray in the Spirit on all occasions with all kinds of prayers and requests. With this in mind, be alert and always keep on praying for all the Lord's people. *Ephesians 6:18*

God chose to allow Abraham and Moses to intercede on behalf of others. Neither determined the ultimate outcome; that is always God's call. In the first instance, ten righteous people were not found, and Sodom and Gomorrah were destroyed. In the second, God reconfirmed with Moses His covenant to make Abraham's descendants His eternal inheritance, for which we, adopted into that inheritance, must be eternally grateful.

Although the exact workings of prayer will remain a mystery during this lifetime, it is no mystery that prayers of intercession are powerful and effective and that Christians are called to pray on behalf of others.

In the days ahead, focus on interceding through prayer on behalf of others. Reflect on times and ways you currently pray for others, as well as ways you might improve. Pray that God will increase your love and concern for others, which will in turn strengthen your desire to pray for them.

For personal reflection and action…

» Think about how you currently pray on behalf of others. Think about ways you can do so more effectively and more often.

» Set a time daily to intercede for others in prayer. Experiment with prompts that remind you when and for whom to pray.

» Start by praying for those who are already upon your heart. Expand your vision to look for those in your path who need your prayers. **Ask** God to bring before you those individuals for whom He would have you pray.

PRAYER MATTER 30

ACTS Helps Balance Prayers

Intercessory prayer was the focus of the last prayer matter, "Does Prayer Change God's Mind?" With my focus on intercession renewed, I have prayed much more regularly for individuals, our church, and all kinds of situations. I have prayed frequently and specifically. I have whenever possible prayed out loud.

> *Balance*—a condition in which different elements are in the correct proportions

These are all very good things, but recently, as I launched right into my prayers of supplication, it occurred to me that in my exuberance I had not been very respectful or loving in approaching God. It reminded me of that occasional time when a grandchild greets me after an absence with, "I need something; can we go to the store and get it?" And I reply, a bit hurt, "Can I at least have a 'hello' and a hug first?"

ACTS is a helpful acronym for achieving balance in regularly scheduled times of prayer.

A doration – Praise God for His attributes–Who He is (His innate character) and what He has done (His mighty acts).

C onfession – Tell God where you have fallen short; ask Him to forgive and remove anything separating you from Him.

T hanksgiving – Thank God for all He has done in your life and through His church. Thank God for Jesus Christ and His saving grace.

S upplication – Humbly petition God where you are led to intercede on behalf of others.

Don't get me wrong. I think God welcomes us whenever we come to Him in prayer. I know I am always glad to see my grandchildren, however each may approach me. But just as children grow with guidance to be more considerate and less self-centered, believers learn as we mature in Christ to balance our supplications with adoration, confession, and thanksgiving. The Lord's Prayer is the prime example of starting not with "Give us our daily bread," but "Hallowed be Thy name."

As eager as we may be to jump into prayers of supplication for others or ourselves, it is important to seek balance in our regular times of prayer. Before launching into requests, take time to meditate on the character of the One to Whom you pray, and praise Him. Don't neglect to confess where you have fallen short, tell God you are sorry, and ask God's forgiveness. Pause to think about all God has done, and thank Him. And then, because Jesus has told us to do so, persist in asking Him for what is on your heart as you intercede on behalf of others and yourself.

For personal reflection and action...

» Practice implementing the ACTS format in your regular prayer time. I have a copy of the above ACTS explanation on the wall of my prayer closet.

» If you are unsure about how to pray any of the specific elements, do a bit of research. For example, for **Adoration,** obtain a list of God's attributes; then reflect on and pray over them (see Prayer Matter 36). Or pray some of the many Psalms or other Scriptures of praise to God.

» As you gain experience in praying through the elements of adoration, confession, thanksgiving, and supplication, be creative and open to ways to expand and enhance each. As always, **ask** God's Spirit to open your heart and to guide you in growing your prayer life.

PRAYER MATTER 31

Prayers of Confession

I often use the ACTS model for praying: Adoration, Confession, Thanksgiving, and Supplication. The confession part, however, I used to cover in a very general way, with my go-to prayers of confession based on the cited segments of Psalms 51 and 139. Although there is definitely a place for these deeply meaningful prayers, I relied on them because I honestly could not think of any sins I had committed that were grievous enough to warrant asking forgiveness. How foolish I was!

My psalm-based prayers are a good example of "be careful what you pray for." While I thought these *were* my prayers of confes-

> Search me, O God, and know my heart; try me, and know my thoughts. See if there be any wicked way in me, and lead me in the way everlasting. *Psalm 139:23–24 (KJV)*

> Create in me a pure heart, O God, and renew a steadfast spirit within me. *Psalm 51:10*

sion, God instead opened my eyes to "wicked ways in me," for which I *should* be asking forgiveness.

The closer I grow to God, and the more I strive to become more Christlike, the more I realize how far short I fall. I once compared myself to other sinners and comparably felt relatively "good." Now, I instead compare myself to Jesus and realize I can never be "good" on my own merit. I once felt okay as long as my actions and words were kind, regardless of how unkind my thoughts might be. Now I understand that unkind thoughts, and other "heart sins," are grievously sinful. Thus, I no longer lack for specifics to confess.

> Whoever conceals their sins does not prosper, but the one who confesses and renounces them finds mercy. *Proverbs 28:13*

> Then I acknowledged my sin to You and did not cover up my iniquity. I said, "I will confess my transgressions to the Lord." And You forgave the guilt of my sin. *Psalm 32:5*

You might think this increased awareness of personal sins would increase the load of personal guilt. But I find, as Scriptures attest, the opposite to be true. As we increasingly recognize, confess, and ask forgiveness for specific sins, barriers fall that stand between us and our Heavenly Father. Like an earthly parent who knows something the child has done and has patiently waited for that child to come clean, God speaks to the repentant heart, "At last, child. Now we can deal with this and you can let it go."

I still pray Psalm 139. But instead of this serving as my general confession, I pray it to ask God to point out additional specific sins He would have me acknowledge and address. I pray Psalm 51 to ask God, after I have acknowledged and confessed those sins, to renew my pureness of heart and steadfastness of spirit. And I find each time, that our faithful Father is merciful to do so.

> If we confess our sins, He is faithful and just and will forgive us our sins and purify us from all unrighteousness.
> *1 John 1:9*

For personal reflection and action...

» Reflect on Scriptures about confession and repentance, such as the ones shared. Take them to heart. Pray over them.

» If you are new to this practice of confession, start by being honest with God. If you are uncomfortable, admit that to God and **ask** for His help. If you are burdened by a sin, state that sin outright and ask forgiveness; remember that your Heavenly Father already knows all about it and has been waiting for you to come to Him. If you have a hard time, as I once did, seeing any sins that need confessing, ask God, through His Holy Spirit, to reveal those to you.

» Resist comparing your "goodness" to that of people in the world around you, because it is tempting to see how much "better" you, relatively, appear to be. Instead, "fix your eyes upon Jesus." Compare yourself only to Jesus Christ; not only does this give us a right view of our own sinfulness, but it also deters our judging others.

Prayer Matter 32

Pray Scriptures Back to God

Our church has an annual Word Marathon, where participants simultaneously read assigned sections of the Bible out loud. Each person reads a different section so that, in just under an hour, God's entire word is prayed in our sanctuary. After one Marathon, three section assignments were left over and sent with folks to complete by reading them aloud at home.

I received one of these home assignments: Exodus 10–21. I smiled at the selection, because I had recently studied the chapters in a Bible study and had subsequently relayed the Exodus account to my grandsons as their action-packed bedtime stories.

As I started my home assignment, I read aloud with lots of inflection, as if telling the story to my grandsons. But it didn't feel like I was praying Scriptures to God. Just then I pictured a kid with her Dad, telling back to him an oft-relayed story of an amazing feat the Dad had once performed. In that context, it seemed natural to substitute "You" for "the Lord." The pronoun shift made the desired connection and turned my reading into a prayer of praise and remembrance spoken directly to God.

When I came to the song of Moses in Exodus 15, I started to quote Moses as written, "I will sing to *the Lord*, for *He* is highly exalted," but immediately I felt compelled to switch back to "*You* are my God, and I will praise *You*." I was delighted to find that apparently Moses shared the feeling, because in verse 6, Moses made exactly the same shift and spoke directly to God for the remaining verses of his song of deliverance. This positive reinforcement even further enhanced my sense of God's presence and of His being pleased to hear His word read back to Him.

The home assignment turned out to be as special as the incredible Word Marathon experience of reading God's word alongside my brothers and sisters in Christ, and I learned a practice that I have continued to use. I encourage you to practice reading back Bible Scriptures to God as you address Him directly. You will be blessed by the results, and I know our Heavenly Father will be pleased.

God, You are my refuge and strength, my ever-present help in trouble. I will not fear, though the earth give way and the mountains fall into the heart of the sea. *From Psalm 46:1–2*

In the morning, Lord, You hear my voice; in the morning I lay my requests before You and wait expectantly. *Psalm 5:3*

God, please help me do everything without grumbling or arguing. Help me be a good example of Your child in a warped generation. Let me shine among them like a star in the sky as I hold firmly to the word of life. *From Philippians 2:14–16*

I praise You, God, Father of our Lord Jesus Christ! You comfort me in all my troubles, so that I can comfort those in any trouble with the comfort that I have received. *From 2 Corinthians 1:3–4*

For personal reflection and action...

» Practice praying Scriptures. Many Scriptures are already written as if addressing God and can be prayed essentially as written. Examples include many of the Psalms and the many prayers of praise interspersed through Paul's epistles in the New Testament. Other Scriptures will need to be adapted into prayer mode.

» Create your own list of Scriptures that are especially meaningful to you, which you can use to prompt your prayers or pray back to God.

» As you implement this practice, you will discover Scriptural prayers suited to all of life's moods and circumstances—from joy to mourning, praise to lament, confidence to fear. God invites you to take everything to Him; **ask** God to help you do so.

Prayer Matter 33

Connecting the Dots Through Scripture and Prayer

Praying Scriptures back to God is a powerful prayer tool. At times, however, a Scripture may seem impossible to apply to a specific circumstance, especially one that is exceedingly difficult. But as we continue seeking God through Scripture, while prayerfully asking Him to teach us, God will help us connect the dots.

Rejoice in the Lord always. Do not be anxious about anything, but in every situation, present your requests to God, and the peace of God will guard your hearts and minds.
Philippians 4:4–7 excerpts

This Scripture has always helped me, Lord. I know it says, "about anything," but surely it cannot apply to this. This is too hard. How can we not be anxious? How could anyone rejoice and feel peace in the midst of this?

Be joyful in hope, patient in affliction, faithful in prayer.
Romans 12:12

May the God of hope fill you with all joy and peace as you trust in Him, so that you may overflow with hope by the power of the Holy Spirit. *Romans 15:13*

Always be prepared to give an answer to everyone who asks you to give the reason for the hope that you have.
1 Peter 3:15b

Another Scripture I try to heed, Lord. I do pray faithfully; I could not make it otherwise. And I strive my best to be patient through affliction. Those are acts I can choose to do. But joy is something I have to feel. How on earth can anyone feel joy in such a circumstance?

Ah, I am beginning to connect the dots, Lord. There is no earthly way to experience joy and peace in this circumstance. But as we seek You through prayer and Scripture, You make it possible. As we make a deliberate choice to trust You, no matter what, You enable us not only to feel joy and peace, but even to overflow with hope through Your power. We do feel hope, Lord. Thank You! How can this be used to further Your purpose?

A Personal Postscript

My son died while I was writing the article on which this prayer matter is based. I wanted to finish it for our church newsletter, but my mind was numbed by grief. Of everything I have written on prayer, these are thoughts I feel God handed me most directly. When I sat down to write, Scriptures came, words flowed, and dots connected. It was weeks before I looked at that newsletter article; when I did, I was encouraged by amazing connections I saw as if for the first time. I pray others who are enduring hard times will experience these same connections.

For personal reflection and action...

» Reflect prayerfully on the above Scriptures. Reflect on the connection between prayer, joy, hope, and peace.

» **Ask** God: To remove your anxiety as you bring your worries to Him; to empower you to rejoice; to give you refreshing glimpses of joy, peace, and hope, even in the midst of hard trials.

» Pray that God will use you as an example to others who need to know the reason for the hope you exhibit, especially in tough times. Prepare your answer and be ready to give it.

PRAYER MATTER 34

Praying Through Tragedy

My heart sank as I watched news reports after a tornado devastated a town and demolished two elementary schools. I had to turn away from images of children being lifted from the rubble. It weighed on me so heavily that at first all I could muster was, "Why, Lord?" It seemed I had no words to pray. Then I realized that I was praying. I was lamenting to God. Instinctively I had turned to Him, like a child to a parent in a bewildering, heartbreaking situation beyond my control.

> "For My thoughts are not your thoughts, neither are your ways My ways," declares the Lord. "As the heavens are higher than the earth, so are My ways higher than your ways and My thoughts than your thoughts." *Isaiah 55:8–9*

God responded, not telling me why, but with reminders that He is always both Sovereign and Good, even when those seem paradoxical. I submitted to the truth that His ways are as much higher than mine as the heavens are higher than the earth. Like Job, I acknowledged that I simply cannot understand. And I prayed, "Please, please have mercy. Lord, help them."

I began to focus on what I do know about God's character and His promises. I looked for signs that even in this tragedy God would work good, and I found many. There were fewer fatalities than feared— far fewer than expected given the extent of devastation. There were instances of remarkable survival. There were examples of courage and compassion. There were stories upon stories of faith in God aired on national and international news.

> Then Job replied to the Lord: "I know that You can do all things; no purpose of Yours can be thwarted. You asked, 'Who is this that obscures My plans without knowledge?' Surely I spoke of things I did not understand, things too wonderful for me to know." *Job 42:1–3*

And so, in such all-too-common occurrences, I pray, "Sovereign Lord, we don't understand tragedies like this. We don't understand why some are miraculously spared and some not. Help us in our questions and grief to trust You and comfort Your people. And let us witness to You, bringing hope where and when it is most needed. We pray in the name of our Savior, Jesus. Amen."

In personal crisis or communal tragedy, this prayer sequence has worked for me:

- Grieve, lament, and question if you are moved to do so. But do it to our Heavenly Father.
- Submit and acknowledge your inability to comprehend. Make the decision to trust God.
- Pray for God's mercy. Intercede earnestly for those impacted.
- Remember God's character and promises. Even in tragedy, look for signs of God's goodness and thank Him.

For personal reflection and action...

» When faced with news of tragedies that bring despair to your heart and tears to your eyes, turn to God. He knows your heart, so be honest with your emotions.

» My prayer sequence is offered as a guideline; adapt as you turn to God to what works best for you.

» It is heartbreaking to watch others suffer and feel powerless to help. Depending on circumstances, we may be able to contribute resources or even provide direct assistance. But, praying is one action we can always take. While, first and foremost, we pray to benefit those suffering, prayer also is a powerful antidote for our own feelings of despair and helplessness, as it involves us in God's workings.

PRAYER MATTER 35

Pray to Walk in Love

Love is a prominent theme throughout the Bible, as we are called first to love God, and second to love our neighbor. The kind of love called for is not just a warm feeling, but active expression. As the apostle Paul put it, we are called to "walk in love."

As we seek to express love actively each day, it is important to recognize the connection between prayer and loving others. Years ago, I read a quote by Richard Foster that I have never forgotten: "If we truly

> Jesus said to him, "'You shall love the Lord your God with all your heart, with all your soul, and with all your mind.' This is the first and great commandment. And the second is like it: 'You shall love your neighbor as yourself.'" *Matthew 22:37–39*

> Therefore be imitators of God, as beloved children. And walk in love, as Christ loved us... *Ephesians 5:1–2a (ESV)*

love people, we will desire for them far more than it is within our power to give them, and this will lead us to prayer. Intercession is a way of loving others."

> "Prayer is to intercede for the well-being of others before God."
> *Augustine*

Those we love most dearly within our families and church are easiest to pray for. Because they are constantly on our minds and hearts, we are motivated frequently to pray for them, especially when their well-being is threatened.

It is more difficult to pray for those who are not so dear, mainly because we are not as naturally motivated and often forget. It is more difficult still to pray for those we don't particularly like.

> And pray in the Spirit on all occasions with all kinds of prayers and requests. With this in mind, be alert and always keep on praying for all the Lord's people. *Ephesians 6:18*

One chapter after the apostle Paul tells us in Ephesians to "walk in love," he tells us always to keep on praying for all the Lord's people. In other words, if we are truly to walk in love, we must intercede regularly for the well-being

> "He prayeth best, who loveth best
> All things both great and small;
> for the dear God who loveth us,
> He made and loveth all."
> *Samuel Taylor Coleridge*

of **all** the above categories of people in our lives.

A good way to start is to pray each day that God increase our love for those both dear and "not so dear," and then pray for them as we are motivated by that love. As our love grows for others, our desire to pray for them will increase. And as we pray more for others, our love for them will increase. What a beautiful cycle!

For personal reflection and action…

» **Ask** God to enlarge your capacity to love and to show you daily how to walk in love. I believe this is one of those prayers that, when prayed with genuine humility and receptivity, God will answer.

> Lord, I want to be more loving,
>
> In my heart, in my heart.
>
> Lord, I want to be more loving,
>
> In my heart.
> *American Folk Hymn*

» As you continue to pray for those you love most dearly, **ask** God to open your heart to others within your circle of life for whom God would have you pray, including those you may not especially like. I suggest creating a list or other prompt to remind you to pray for those folks.

» **Pray!** Pray often for your expanded circle of the Lord's people. Expect God to answer, and be watching for ways your love for others begins to grow.

PRAYER MATTER 36

Pray God's Attributes

How do you get to know someone? You spend time with that person. You converse and listen. You get to know the person's character as you observe actions and qualities exhibited in various roles.

If this leads to admiration and trust, your relationship and communication deepen. The better you know someone in a positive way, the more effectively you communicate. And the more effectively you communicate, the better acquainted you want to and are able to become.

> "And this is eternal life, that they know You the only true God, and Jesus Christ whom You have sent." *John 17:3*

> "Let us occupy ourselves entirely in knowing God. The more we know Him, the more we will desire to know Him."
> *Brother Lawrence*

So it is in our relationship with God. The more we pray and spend time with God, the better we get to know Him. The better we get to know God, the more effective, natural, and intimate our prayers become.

An excellent way to know God better is to learn about, reflect on, and praise God for His attributes. God's attributes are inherent qualities that God reveals about Himself. He reveals Himself in the Bible through interactions with His creation. God reveals Himself to humankind and to each individual through the observed and experienced world.

Research God's attributes, and reflect on each. Doing so will expand your knowledge of God. It will also strengthen your prayers as you are better enabled to pray God's attributes.

The better you know God, the more you will stand in awe of our majestic, sovereign Lord. You will praise Him more often, spontaneously, and perfectly. As you grasp more and more God's infinite power, omniscience, and goodness, the more you will respect, love, and trust Him, and the more certain you will become that God, Who knows the end from the beginning, is assuredly capable of keeping every promise He has made.

> I make known the end from the beginning, from ancient times, what is still to come. I say, "My purpose will stand, and I will do all that I please." *Isaiah 46:10*

Ask God to reveal His character to you. Expect this to be one of those prayers that God will answer with "Yes!" Make praying God's attributes a central part of your prayer life.

**Example:
Infinite,
Creator,
All-Knowing**

Do you not know? Have you not heard? The Lord is the everlasting God, the Creator of the ends of the earth. He will not grow tired or weary, and His understanding, no one can fathom. *Isaiah 40:28*

God, I acknowledge that I cannot begin to fathom Your attributes. Yet, with my whole heart, I praise You that You are the everlasting God and Creator. I am so grateful that while I grow tired and weary, You do not; You are always there to help and sustain me. In this confusing world filled with conflicting information, teach me to rely on You for understanding. Reveal more of Yourself to me; help me grasp Your eternal majesty. I pray in Jesus' name. Amen.

For personal reflection and action...

» Research and compile a list of God's attributes. Practice incorporating God's attributes in your prayers until it becomes a routine part of your prayer life.

» Praise God each day for one of His attributes. For example, God is Creator. As you pray for loved ones, thank God for creating each of them. Thank God for creating every blessing you enjoy. As you observe the natural world, thank God for the beauty of the earth, for the beauty of the skies.

» Pray God's attributes in your supplications. If you worry about unsettling events, call upon God's sovereignty. If you fear for loved ones, entrust them to our faithful, good, and loving God.

» Direct others toward God by using His attributes in praying with them. For example, pray at mealtime, "Lord God, You are the Creator. You created and care for us. Thank You for providing this meal."

» **Ask** God to point You to His attributes and to reveal more of Himself to you.

Prayer Matter 37

Bedtime Prayers

The first prayers I ever prayed were at bedtime. From earliest memory, I recall praying every night as a child. I would start with the simple poem on the right and then add blessings. The blessing part covered my parents, sisters, and all the dogs we ever owned.

For years as I grew older, bedtime remained my primary time for prayer. The negative side of praying only at bedtime was that my prayers were typically shallow, always one-sided, and often I went to

"Now I lay me down to sleep; I pray the Lord my soul to keep. If I should die before I wake, I pray the Lord my soul to take. God bless Mother and Daddy and Sandra and Jan and Mugsy and Teddy and Rascal." *My childhood prayer at bedtime*

"Prayer should be the key of the day and the lock of the night." *C. H. Spurgeon*

sleep mid-prayer. On the positive side, the familiarity of the simple prayers calmed my worries and fears, brought me to God every single night, and closed each day with thoughts of God.

I still pray at bedtime, but my overall prayer life is more balanced. I appreciate the unique benefits of morning prayer to start each day afresh with God. I value time during the day to practice the listening side of prayer. In an effort to "pray continually," I speak to God whenever a worry or thought or gratitude prompts me. But I still turn my mind to God one last time by praying before I fall asleep every night. And those times when I am tired, weary, or downcast—times when I cannot seem to form words as I lay in bed, it is second nature to revert to a simple childhood prayer that brings comfort and sweet memories.

If you make a habit of praying at bedtime, may it continue to bring you nightly peace and closeness to your Heavenly Father. If not, I encourage you to give it a try every night for a month. While bedtime prayers may not be your deepest or most eloquent, they will yield rich blessings.

A Personal Postscript

Any time I am with my grandchildren during bedtime, I pray with them. Sometimes I use my childhood poem; while it never bothered me to pray, "If I

> "Now I lay me down to sleep; I pray the Lord my soul to keep. Watch o'er me as I sleep this night, and wake me with the morning light."

should die before I wake…," I adapt as shown. Most times, however, I place my hand on my grandchild's head and pray a blessing, then have the child simply talk to God, and end with a goodnight kiss.

For personal reflection and action...

» Pray at bedtime. Whether you prefer an extended time of prayer just before getting in bed, choose to kneel beside your bed, or just pray a simple prayer in bed as you close your eyes for sleep, make it your habit to pray each night.

» At times, my husband and I hold hands in bed before going to sleep and pray together out loud. We especially do this when we are worried. Not only are we thus able to pray longer and more deeply without falling asleep, but it helps release our worries to God and bring more restful sleep. An added benefit is the sweet intimacy Mike and I experience as we pray together this final prayer of the day.

» If you are with a child at bedtime, always take the opportunity to pray. Work to develop the habit of bedtime prayer in your children, grandchildren, or others.

» Examples of bedtime prayers are readily available. Books of bedtime prayers make excellent gifts for children or adults. Or print online prayers and affix to index cards or make into bookmarks, so they will be handy at bedtime.

Prayer Matter 38

When You Are Overwhelmed

In the midst of our son's cancer battle, I found myself one day on the brink of despair over an out-of-control prayer list. As I muttered, "God help me," an Old Testament Scripture came to mind, in which King Hezekiah took a threatening letter that was delivered from an overwhelmingly powerful enemy and spread it out before the Lord. (Read Isaiah 37:14–20.)

> Hezekiah read the letter. Then he went up to the temple of the Lord and spread it out before the Lord. And Hezekiah prayed to the Lord: "Lord Almighty, the God of Israel, enthroned between the cherubim, You alone are God over all the kingdoms of the earth. You have made heaven and earth. Give ear, Lord, and hear; open Your eyes, Lord, and see; listen to… It is true, Lord, that… Now, Lord our God, deliver us… so that all the kingdoms of the earth may know that You, Lord, are the only God." *Isaiah 37:14–20, excerpted*

I dropped to my knees and mentally spread all my prayer concerns before God, specifically, one by one. I began with, "Lord, I am feeling overwhelmed," and then proceeded to cite specific names and details regarding children and grandchildren, friends, relatives, church members, as well as general concerns. My concerns ranged from very serious to relatively petty, but they cumulatively were wearing on me.

After I laid out all this, I acknowledged before God that while I was overwhelmed, I knew He never was. I praised God's Sovereignty and asked Him to take charge of each concern. Releasing each request to God, I prayed, "I trust You, God."

As I took a few deep breaths in silence, the melody and words our choral group had sung to senior citizens that morning sprang into my head, "When upon life's billows you are tempest tossed, when you are discouraged, thinking all is lost, count your many blessings, name them one by one, and it will surprise you what the Lord has done."

So, I proceeded to do so, thanking God for each blessing related to a person or situation on my list. For instance, with David, I thanked God for bringing him through teenage trials to being an amazing teacher with a precious family and for bringing him through two cycles of cancer and treatment. I was struck by God's grace that the worst of both treatments had occurred during summers, enabling him to continue teaching through both school years. In the face of fears for him and others, as I similarly thanked God for each blessing, I recalled a flood of past storms where God's grace had been evident, and I was once

P.S. Be sure to read the remainder of Isaiah 37 to find out how the overwhelming threat over which Hezekiah prayed is resolved.

again reassured that God's grace would be sufficient for whatever trials lay ahead. I stood up, with my heart redirected.

When your prayer list is overwhelming...

» Stop, and turn to God.

» Tell God how you are feeling. Tell your Heavenly Father you need His help.

» Praise God for His attributes. As you acknowledge, for example, God's sovereignty and power, you not only honor Him, but you also remind yourself that God is infinitely capable to handle anything.

» Lay each and every concern before God, and **ask** Him to take charge.

» Imagine yourself releasing each concern to God. As you do, say, "I trust You, God."

» Consider going an extra step to recount blessings related to persons or situations on your list. This is a powerful way to change your perspective from despair to hope. Once I start looking for blessings, God brings to mind many blessings I had not previously recognized. And I am reassured that God's grace, which has brought us thus far, will lead us home.

Prayer Matter 39

Learning to Be Still

I recall a sermon about silently seeking God's presence. The preacher told of a boy training his dog to ignore distractions by learning his master's voice. It was a simple and powerful example, which rang true in light of Scripture and personal experience.

> My sheep listen to my voice; I know them, and they follow me. *John 10:27*

Although I know prayer involves both speaking and listening to God (see Prayer Matter 13), I still struggle with the discipline of listening, in silence, for God's voice. So I determined daily to try.

I selected a quiet spot. Having decided to start small with ten minutes, I set my phone timer. Taking a deep breath, I tried to still my mind and listen for God. What I heard was a storm of thoughts. Over and over I tried to push back distracting thoughts and settle into silence. Finally I checked my timer, thinking I had failed to turn it on, only to discover it had been seven minutes. I realized this would not be easy.

> "And as I listened and slowly learned to obey and shut my ears to every sound, I found after a while that when the other voices ceased, or I ceased to hear them, there was a still, small voice in the depths of my being that began to speak with an inexpressible tenderness, power and comfort." *A. B. Simpson, The Holy Spirit, Power from On High*

I continue this practice of training to be calm. I counter the pull of other voices by praying Scriptures such as "God teach me, and I will be quiet." I imagine God gently saying, "Just be still." I have been rewarded with gentle nudges of the Spirit not only during that quiet time, but also more discernibly throughout the day as I pray regarding other matters.

> Be still and know that I am God. *Psalm 46:10a*

> Teach me and I will be quiet; show me where I have been wrong. *Job 6:24*

If you do not practice seeking God's voice through external and internal silence, I lovingly invite you to join me in learning to do so. I long for each of us to achieve the experience of A.B. Simpson, who wrote in *The Holy Spirit, Power from On High*, "As I listened, it became to me the voice of prayer...and I did not need to think so hard, or pray so hard, or trust so hard; but that 'still small voice' of the Holy Spirit in my heart was God's prayer in my secret soul, God's answer to all my questions, God's life and strength—the living GOD Himself as my Life and my All."

Centering Down

It is often hard to center down to listen, to quiet all the busy thoughts that clamor for attention in order to become still in God's presence.

One technique for centering down is to use a prayer man-

- Jesus Prayer: "Lord Jesus, Son of God, have mercy on me, a sinner."
- Father, I adore You. Jesus, I adore You. Spirit, I adore You.
- Lord, help me love You. Lord, help me know You. Lord, help me hear You.

tra. Search "prayer mantra" online to learn more, but it basically is repeating a phrase in prayer, preferably while inhaling and exhaling with intentional, focused breathing.

Some phrases I have used are shown. It is easy to develop your own adaptations. Just keep it simple and pray from your heart.

For personal reflection and action…

» As you train to be still before God, begin by praying for God to teach you to be quiet.

» Expect Him to do so, and follow God's prompts, which may differ from the ones I followed.

» Keep practicing. Even great people of prayer, as quoted from A.B. Simpson, "slowly learned to obey."

PRAYER MATTER 40

Sacrifice of Thanksgiving

As often occurs when God is teaching me something, the terms "sacrifice of thanksgiving" and "thank offerings" recently showed up in multiple Scriptures and writings that happened across my path in the same week. While I was aware of the Old Testament basis for the term "thank offerings," use of "sacrifice of thanksgiving" caught my attention and led me to reflect on what it means to me.

> Sacrifice thank offerings to God; fulfill your vows to the Most High... Those who sacrifice thank offerings honor Me... *Psalm 50:14, 23a*

I typically think of giving thanks as a joyful response to a kindness or gift. I witness and practice this kind of gratitude often. It comes easy and flows naturally.

Sacrifice would seem not to fit this scenario. Sacrifice entails loss; true sacrifice involves not just giving up something, but something we will really miss. Intentional sacrifice does not come easily or flow naturally. How is thanksgiving a sacrifice?

The psalmist tells us to sacrifice thank offerings to God. Any time we give thanks to God in response to obvious blessings, it is an offering to our Creator, and I know He is pleased. But I don't think that is the sacrificial offering to which the psalmist refers.

> Let them praise the Lord for His great love and for the wonderful things He has done for them. Let them offer sacrifices of thanksgiving and sing joyfully about His glorious acts.
> *Psalm 107:21–22 (NLT)*

Think of times you have not felt like giving thanks—times when things were not going well. Perhaps you have experienced

> Rejoice always, pray continually, give thanks in all circumstances; for this is God's will for you in Christ Jesus.
> *1 Thessalonians 5:16–18*

great loss, struggled physically or financially, or endured troubled relationships. Maybe you have been deeply depressed or just generally grumpy.

Joyful, spontaneous thanksgiving does not flow naturally at those times. Yet it is precisely in such circumstances that giving thanks to God becomes a thank offering. It goes against the grain; it costs us. It requires submitting to God's sovereignty and believing in His goodness even we are hurting. At those times, a thank offering truly becomes a sacrifice of thanksgiving.

The results are too many to enumerate. But for starters, God is honored. As we yield to God, we allow His Spirit to work more freely within us. As we acknowledge God's glorious acts, we find reason to rejoice, even when we struggle.

And gradually it becomes more and more natural for us, like the apostle Paul, to give thanks in all circumstances.

A Personal Postscript

The sacrifice of thanksgiving is very personal for me. Read more in Prayer Matter 47 about a prayer journal I have kept since our son died, in which I thank God for many, many things pertaining to David. While it was easy to thank God for many good memories of my son, as I forced myself to seek aspects of hard memories for which to give thanks, God comforted my heart and changed my perspective.

For personal reflection and action...

» Reflect for yourself on what it means to offer sacrifices of thanksgiving to God. **Ask** God to grant insight.
» Make gratitude your goal for the next weeks, and be intentional to express thanks to God often each day.
» Watch especially for times when you do not "feel" like giving thanks, and make a point to thank God in spite of your worries or circumstances. It is precisely at those times that you develop the practice of offering sacrifices of thanksgiving to God.

PRAYER MATTER 41

Pray Without Ceasing

In 1 Thessalonians 5:17, the apostle Paul tells us to "Pray without ceasing." This teaching has always intrigued me. What does it

> Pray without ceasing...
> *1 Thessalonians 5:17*

mean to pray without ceasing? How can we possibly pray continually?

As I understand it, to pray without ceasing refers to living our daily lives in a continual attitude of prayer—maintaining ongoing interaction with the Father as we go about our business.

This occurs most readily during needy times in life, like when loved ones or we ourselves are in crisis. Intensely aware of our helplessness and desperate for God's help, we are driven to dialogue privately but continually with Him as we stumble through each day. The challenge is to develop that continual connection with God when our lives are on a more even keel, as we go through our daily routine, but busy, tasks.

As I pondered that challenge, it occurred to me that I talk to myself all the time—even, at times, out loud. In fact, no one talks to me as much as I talk to myself. So, I began more consciously to include God in my internal conversation. Soon, I found myself talking to God about pretty much everything.

With God in my inner thoughts, He has become the One to whom I express awe when I am surprised by the beauty of an evening sunset. He is the One to whom I first turn when fear jumps unexpectedly into my path. Building up my courage while waiting to see the doctor, I ask God to help me ask the right questions and surface any issues needing treatment.

> We talk to ourselves all the time, and often out loud. Why not include God in the conversation?

> "While your hands are busy with the world, let your hearts still talk with God." *C. H. Spurgeon*

Becoming impatient while waiting at a traffic light, I redirect my internal voice to thank God that I have my own car and for the independence that brings. Growing annoyed at the slow person checking out in front of me, I tell myself how blessed I am to be in a country with so many stores and that I have money to spend, and I ask God to bless the person holding up the line.

You get the idea. No one talks to you as much as you do to yourself. Try being more intentional to include God regularly in that conversation, and ask God to help you do so.

For personal reflection and action…

» As you pray more and more frequently and employ more prayer practices, more continual communication with your Heavenly Father will evolve naturally. But if your goal is truly to pray without ceasing, **ask** God to help you, and then be intentional to pray continually.

> P.S. It is wise to remember that you should never be in a place or in an internal conversation that you would not want God to be part of.

» Be more aware of your ongoing internal conversation, and make a focused effort to include God as you begin talking to Him about everything.

» Specifically invite God each morning to join in your conversation that day, and pray for the Holy Spirit to bolster that connection.

PRAYER MATTER 42

Join with Heaven in Praising God

In Revelation 4, Jesus Christ calls John up to Heaven to show him dramatic visions of coming judgments that "must take place." But first, John is given fearfully awesome glimpses of God sitting on His throne, surrounded by beings who glorify and worship Him.

Take time to read and reflect on this chapter. May it remind you that as we live our lives on earth and experience daily joys, griefs, hopes, and

Day and night they never stop saying:

"Holy, holy, holy is the Lord God Almighty,

Who was, and is, and is to come." *Revelation 4:8b*

They lay down their crowns before the throne and say:
"You are worthy, our Lord and God,
To receive glory and honor and power,
For You created all things,
And by Your will they were created
And have their being."
Revelation 4:10b–11

fears, beyond the veil of our sight is a heavenly realm where God already reigns eternally. God is right now sitting on His throne, and all of Heaven worships Him.

If we truly grasp that, it will reorient the way we live. And we will intuitively respond like the beings John saw, giving glory, honor, and thanks to God as we worship the One who is worthy to receive glory and honor and power.

Truly, we are never closer to Heaven than when we praise God while simultaneously imagining the heavenly worship that is ongoing over our heads. As Charles Spurgeon noted, praise is in fact the rehearsal of our eternal song. Let's make it a good rehearsal!

> "Praise is the rehearsal of our eternal song. By grace we learn to sing, and in glory we continue to sing." *C. H. Spurgeon*

Prayer Challenge: Praise!

I try always to start prayers with praise, but all too quickly I go from "Hallowed be Thy name," to "give me this day my

> "Glory to God in the highest heaven, and on earth peace to those on whom His favor rests." *Luke 2:14*

daily bread…" and everything else on my prayer list.

These next weeks, try setting aside time each day solely to "give glory to God in the highest." Revelation 4:8 and 4:11 are good Scriptures to launch prayers, as are many Psalms. Just praise God and picture yourself joining with ongoing worship in Heaven during this time.

Refrain from moving into prayer requests right after; just let your praise linger. Certainly, bring intercessory prayers and worries before God daily—but at another sitting. I suspect after we have spent time in focused praise, our other requests will shift in perspective.

For personal reflection and action...

» Strive to be more intentional about starting prayers with praise—not as a precursory prelude to the "main business" of your petitions, but in genuine, worshipful awe of our majestic Creator and sovereign God.

» If you feel at times like you are praising God out of respect or routine and not from the heart, pause and **ask** God to give you a heart for praise. But meantime, keep praising. God honors our obedience, and often, the heart catches up to right actions.

» Incorporate Scriptures, songs, and doxologies to enhance your offerings of praise. Words of praise written by God's people through the ages are an excellent way to expand our praise vocabulary. Read and reflect on them; pray them to God.

Prayer Matter 43

Carry Each Other's Burdens

A friend and I taught a children's lesson from Mark 2:1–12 about four friends who carried their paralyzed friend to Jesus to be healed. The focus Scripture for the lesson was Galatians 6:2, "Carry each other's burdens."

> A few days later, when Jesus again entered Capernaum, the people heard that he had come home. They gathered in such large numbers that there was no room left, not even outside the door, and he preached the word to them. Some men came, bringing to him a paralyzed man, carried by four of them. Since they could not get him to Jesus because of the crowd, they made an opening in the roof above Jesus by digging through it and then lowered the mat the man was lying on… So he said to the man, "I tell you, get up, take your mat and go home." He got up, took his mat and walked out in full view of them all. This amazed everyone and they praised God, saying, "We have never seen anything like this!" *Mark 2:1–4; 11–12*

We helped the children understand what burdens are and how some things can weigh people down. They brainstormed things that could burden people—from hurt feelings to sickness to having someone you love die. We were surprised and touched by how many children in our midst were experiencing firsthand very difficult burdens within their families.

Then we asked the children to suggest ways we can help carry burdens for a friend who is feeling weighed down. They offered remarkably good suggestions, but we were especially moved by the response of one preschooler, "You can carry your friend to Jesus." When asked how they could do that, the group response was, "You can pray for them." What a powerful and precious picture this provides of intercessory prayer!

A common challenge when praying is how to maintain focus and not become distracted. One tool to counter distractions is using your voice.

> Carry each other's burdens, and in this way you will fulfill the law of Christ. *Galatians 6:2*

Praying aloud is a very effective way to help stay engaged and prevent random thoughts from interrupting our conversations with God.

> Then people brought little children to Jesus for him to place his hands on them and pray for them. But the disciples rebuked them. Jesus said, "Let the little children come to me, and do not hinder them, for the Kingdom of Heaven belongs to such as these." *Matthew 19:13–14*

Another effective prayer tool is applying our imaginations—picturing things in our minds as we pray. So, as we pray for individuals, what if we picture literally carrying them to Jesus? If you are praying for someone who is physically or mentally sick, picture carrying and laying that person before Jesus as did the friends in our children's story. If you are praying for children, picture bringing them for Jesus to take upon his lap as when he said, "Let the little children come to me." Then, pray aloud to Jesus for the person on your mind and heart.

You get the picture! Now, practice creatively adding your own mental images as you pray for those in your life who need to be carried to Jesus.

For personal reflection and action…

» As you pray for an individual, picture in your mind carrying or lifting up that person to Jesus. Then request what is on your heart on behalf of the individual.

» As you pray, hand over to God your own burdens about the situation. If you are fearful, tell God you are afraid, **ask** God to help you, and tell God you trust Him.

» Infuse into your prayers such Scriptures as those on this page. For example, "Lord, as the men in Capernaum carried their friend to Jesus, I lift up my friend to You in prayer." Or, "Lord, You have told us to carry each other's burdens. Please show me how I can best help carry the heavy burden that is currently weighing down my loved one."

» **Ask** the Holy Spirit to inspire your imagination as you pray for others.

Prayer Matter 44

Prayer of Saint Francis

We can learn much from the prayers of others, whether Bible characters or notable servants of God through history.

> Lord, make me an instrument of Your peace.
> Where there is hatred, let me sow love;
> where there is injury, pardon;
> where there is doubt, faith;
> where there is despair, hope;
> where there is darkness, light;
> and where there is sadness, joy.
>
> O Divine Master, grant that I may not so much seek
> to be consoled as to console;
> to be understood as to understand;
> to be loved as to love.
> For it is in giving that we receive;
> it is in pardoning that we are pardoned;
> and it is in dying that we are born to eternal life.
> Amen.

One such individual is Saint Francis of Assisi. The name of Saint Francis is associated so closely with humility and compassion for the poor that in 2013, Jorge Mario Bergoglio launched his papacy by assuming the name Pope Francis I.

The prayer attributed to Saint Francis of Assisi is one of the most beautiful and selfless prayers of history. It is a powerful and much-needed antidote in a world that seems increasingly focused on self and "What's in it for me and mine?"

Reflect on the Prayer of Saint Francis. Pray it. Reflect on the quoted Scriptures. In the weeks ahead, **ask** God to show you how to live into this prayer. **Ask** God to make you an instrument of His peace.

> "Blessed are the peacemakers, for they will be called children of God." *Matthew 5:9*

> "For I was hungry and you gave me something to eat, I was thirsty and you gave me something to drink, I was a stranger and you invited me in, I needed clothes and you clothed me, I was sick and you looked after me, I was in prison and you came to visit me."
> *Matthew 25:35–36*

Do nothing out of selfish ambition or vain conceit. Rather, in humility value others above yourselves, not looking to your own interests but each of you to the interests of others. *Philippians 2:3–4*

"For even the Son of Man did not come to be served, but to serve, and to give his life as a ransom for many." *Mark 10:45*

Then Jesus said to his disciples, "Whoever wants to be my disciple must deny themselves and take up their cross and follow me. For whoever wants to save their life will lose it, but whoever loses their life for me will find it." *Matthew 16:24–25*

For personal reflection and action...

» Seek a quiet place and pray the Prayer of Saint Francis. Do it regularly over the next weeks, and be alert to the difference it makes in your outlook and in your relationships.

» Reflect on Jesus' teachings from related Scriptures. **Ask** God to teach you and touch you with the truth reflected therein.

» Look for opportunities to live into the selflessness expressed in this prayer.

PRAYER MATTER 45

Pray and Fast

Fasting is not commonly practiced today. For this reason, in addition to my limited experience, I had not planned to include the topic in these prayer matters. However, after prayerful consideration, I deemed it important to include. I have also determined to reinstate my personal practice, which I have neglected the past several years.

A primary reason for fasting is strong Biblical precedent;

> *Fasting*: Abstaining from food or drink for a period of time, in this case for spiritual purposes. We can also fast from other worldly things central to daily life.

fasting was commonly practiced in both the Old and New Testaments. Reasons Bible characters fasted include purification, repentance, clarity of discernment, and focused pleas for God's mercy, protection, and deliverance.

Even more significant, Jesus himself fasted. And when he taught his disciples, Jesus' wording assumed that they fasted; in Matthew 6:16, Jesus said, "**when** you fast," not "if".

Examples and purposes of fasts in the Bible:

- Moses receiving the 10 Commandments *(Exodus 34:28)* – Sanctification for God's presence; to hear God clearly
- Israel's army prior to battle *(Judges 20:26)* – Deliverance from enemies
- King David pleading for the life of his son *(2 Samuel 12:16–17)* – Intervention; mercy
- Daniel praying over the desolation of Jerusalem *(Daniel 9:2–3)* – Mercy for the nation
- Jesus during his wilderness temptation *(Matthew 4:2–4)* – Spiritual strength; protection
- Paul and Barnabus installing church leaders *(Acts 14:23)* – Discernment; consecration

While fasting, physical desires are pushed aside for a set period of time in order to honor God. Fasting shows humility and acknowledges dependence on God; it demonstrates that we value Him above physical urges. Fasting enables us to draw nearer to God, speak to God more attentively, and hear God's voice more clearly. Fasting takes our focus off the things of the world to focus on God.

At a challenging time in my earlier life, I routinely fasted to counteract worldly pressures. In later life, I have primarily fasted when called to make a crucial decision with no clear alternative, or when a loved one has been in immediate and desperate need of protection or deliverance. I, along with many others, currently feel called to fast and pray for God's intervention and mercy upon our nation.

Fasting greatly facilitates ability to "pray continually" (*1 Thessalonians 5:17*). When abstaining from food, every time I feel the nudge of appetite, I remember why I am fasting and am prompted to pray.

Fasting also draws me closer to God. Jesus tells us to fast in secret, so when I fast, I tell no one except—for practical reasons—my husband. Thus, throughout the predetermined period of fasting, it is as if God and I share a secret, which makes my conversation with God especially sacred.

Fasting requires discipline. It requires sacrifice. It goes against urges of the flesh. And for precisely those reasons, it has unique potential to connect us to God in focused and powerful ways.

If you have not tried fasting, I encourage you to give it a try. If, like me, you have fallen out of practice, I invite you to join me in reinstating the discipline. May God bless our efforts.

For personal reflection and action...

» First, pray about fasting. **Ask** God to nudge you if, why, and how to fast.

» Recognize that you can fast in various ways, for varying periods of time. I have fasted for 36 hours—from supper, through the next day, to breakfast the following morning; for 24 hours—from breakfast to breakfast; or a partial day—from breakfast to supper. I drink only water.

» Try also fasting from things other than food or drink. Examples include television, electronic devices, and video games. This provides a good option if medical or other factors preclude fasting from food or drink. Or, try fasting from specific food or drink you tend to crave, such as sweets or soft drinks. Whenever you experience craving for the thing from which you are abstaining, turn instead to God.

» Be intentional during your time of fasting to listen to God's voice and spend time with Him.

PRAYER MATTER 46

Pray to Be FED by God

Adversity can either shut us down or motivate us to rely on God. I have experienced both since the death of David. In early days after my son died, I basically functioned one step at a time, one foot in front of the other. I learned to direct my focus to one small task at a time—literally, as in telling myself, "Wash your face. Now, put on your makeup. Now, get dressed…"

> "Life is short; we make it still shorter by the careless waste of time." *Victor Hugo*

I manage much better now, but lethargy can still be an issue; I still battle days of feeling adrift. When I do, I would prefer to curl up in bed or play a mindless video game on my smartphone for hours to pass time and ignore my aching heart. At the end of those days, I lie down regretting that I wasted precious time.

> Lord, be gracious to us; we long for You. Be our strength every morning, our salvation in time of distress. *Isaiah 33:2*

The days I fare best in this battle are those days that begin with God. On those days, I start by telling God how off-balance I am feeling, and how desperately I need to be FED by Him. Then, I pray for God's Holy Spirit to give me the focus, energy, and discernment needed to complete the work God would have me do that day. As needed, I repeat my petition through the day—for focus, energy, and discernment. At the end of those days, I lie down thanking God for what He enabled me to get done.

> **Pray to be FED by God:**
> **Focus, Energy, Discernment**
> *May Your Holy Spirit give me **focus** and **energy** to do what You would have me do this day, and the **discernment** to know just what it is You would have me do.*

We all need daily to be FED by God. Like the Israelites in the desert, the spiritual manna we receive today will not carry forward to tomorrow. Whether you currently are experiencing hard times, or even if you are experiencing an interlude of relative calm in your life journey, you need God's strength to live to the fullest. Make it a point to pray each morning over the next weeks to be FED by God every day. Lay your request before your Heavenly Father, and expect Him to hear and respond.

> In the morning, Lord, you hear my voice; in the morning I lay my requests before you and wait expectantly. *Psalm 5:3*

For personal reflection and action...

» Start each day by **asking** for God's Holy Spirit to give you the focus, energy, and discernment needed to complete God's work for you that day.

» Then, tell God you trust Him, and turn the day over to Him.

> Let us throw off everything that hinders and the sin that so easily entangles. And let us run with perseverance the race marked out for us, fixing our eyes on Jesus, the pioneer and perfecter of faith.
> *Hebrews 12:1b–2a*

» These practices are keys to fruitful living in both the hard and easier times of life. In times of adversity, you are most keenly aware that you cannot manage on your own; you absolutely need God's strength to function effectively.

» In times of prosperity, you may think you are managing fine, only to find yourself having drifted from God due to busyness and other distractions that prevent you from fixing your eyes on Jesus.

Prayer Matter 47

Give Thanks in All Circumstances

Rejoice, pray, and give thanks. These are simple and straight-forward admonitions. Practicing them should be easy enough, right?

Well, except maybe for the adverbs—always, continually, and in all circumstances. Those qualifiers add a whole new dimension to each practice. Take thanksgiving: how can we possibly give thanks in all circumstances?

> Rejoice always, pray continually, give thanks in all circumstances; for this is God's will for you in Christ Jesus.
> *1 Thess. 5:16–18*

When our son died just prior to Thanksgiving 2012, a dear friend shared something that helped her after her daughter's death—writing down

> Give thanks to the Lord, for He is good; His love endures forever.
> *Psalm 106:1*

things for which she was thankful in relation to the child she missed so much.

Although I could see little for which to thank God in these circumstances, I was motivated to try. I identified one thing for which I was thankful in relation to David, wrote my thanks to God, and felt a first glimmer of joy. That led to another thankful prayer, and then another.

> The more we give thanks, the more blessings we find for which to give thanks.

Circumstances did not change, nor did grief go away, but God granted a new perspective. The gratitude journal became a game-changer, as God revealed in hindsight His grace and mercy even in the worst of circumstances.

> Through the lens of gratitude, we learn to see God's grace and mercy in all circumstances.

Note that the apostle Paul did not say give thanks *for* all circumstances. There are many circumstances in this broken world that we should rightly abhor. But we absolutely can give thanks *in* all circumstances by choosing to look beyond even the worst to focus on God's goodness, mercy, and grace.

> Do not focus on what you lack or have lost. Rather, be thankful for what you have and are promised as God's child.

Make it a priority to do just that in these coming weeks. Please join me in praying that for each of us. Then, find a way to remind yourself daily.

For personal reflection and action…

» Memorize 1 Thessalonians 5:16–18. Recite it often to yourself, and pray it as a frequent prayer. "Lord, help me this day to rejoice always, pray continually, and give thanks in all circumstances. Empower me to do Your will."

» Find something each day for which specially to thank God. It

Holy Spirit, teach us in the coming weeks how better to rejoice, pray, and give thanks. Not haphazardly, but always, continually, and in all circumstances. May we become increasingly thankful. Help us focus not on what we lack or have lost, but on what we have and are promised as Your children. Above all, we thank You for Christ, our eternal hope. We pray in Jesus' name. Amen.

may be helpful to record your thanks in a journal, calendar, or smartphone app. Writing it out not only helps you identify and articulate blessings, but it provides a record to which you can refer when you need reminders of God's past blessings.

» When you find yourself hung up on a particular trial, fear, or loss, **ask** God to change your perspective and show you something about the situation for which to be thankful. **Ask** God to give you a heart to recognize and be thankful for what you do have, rather than focus on what you do not have.

PRAYER MATTER 48

Praying Over the Unthinkable

Many awful things happen in this world that I do not want to think about. Examples of such awful things include missing and kidnapped children, human trafficking, women and children captured and brutally enslaved, Christians imprisoned and tortured by evil regimes, and Christians beheaded.

When it comes to praying over these things, I find it very difficult. Why, I wonder, is it so hard for me to pray for people in situations who most desperately need God's intervention?

I think partly it is so hard because I would rather not even approach these situations in my thoughts. I just cannot bear to go there. It is emotionally paralyzing; I am unable to bear the thoughts and images associated with each situation. It is partly fear. I cannot even begin to think of someone I love enduring such suffering, and I would rather bury the fact that such things even happen.

For a long time, when I approached praying over unthinkable situations, I found my thoughts blocked. After hearing the latest "unthinkable," I would typically pray a simple, "Dear God, please help her/him/them." Knowing that God hears every prayer, I believe each simple prayer did make a difference. However, I well knew that I was not praying with the depth, focus, and intent with which I pray over other matters.

God, forgive me for lacking courage even to think about a situation that this person at this very moment is having to experience. Help me set my own vicarious emotions aside, so I can pray effectively for this person. Forgive me for essentially thinking that this situation is too awful even for You to redeem. Help me remember that, surely, Your arm is not too short. Lord, I beg You:

- *Wrap Your arms right now around this person. Let her feel Your presence, Your comfort, Your hope.*
- *Grant him respite this evening, Lord. Let him rest in Your supernatural peace.*
- *Turn the hearts of her captors to show favor and mercy.*
- *Fill him with Your Spirit; connect him with the Lord Jesus.*
- *Through Your supernatural power, give her strength to endure, and give her assurance of eternal life beyond this temporal suffering.*
- *Let him know that he is not forgotten, that others are praying for him at this moment.*
- *Empower her to be Your witness, as her captors see her faith and Your favor.*
- *And if he is to die, grant a vision of Heaven that overshadows fear and pain.*

So, I **asked** God to help me pray for those subjected to unthinkable suffering. Immediately, the thought surfaced that I had not been trusting God—as if some situations were too irredeemable even for Him. I recalled my relief as a parent when my child sheepishly came to me in desperation, with a problem he thought I couldn't handle hearing about. Putting myself in the position of a child, I simply began telling God what was in my heart.

Gradually, I am learning to pray more faithfully and specifically over awful situations. My trust in God has expanded. As I imagine my prayers joined with those of many others, I picture Jesus intervening. I look forward in Heaven to learning the full extent to which the prayers of God's people have impacted the unthinkable.

> Surely the arm of the Lord is not too short to save, nor His ear too dull to hear. *Isaiah 59:1*

For personal reflection and action...

» Tell God what is in your heart.
» Admit how hard it is to pray about this. Confess your limited trust in God. Confess your own lack of courage in "going there."
» Tell God you desperately want Him to help those who are suffering unthinkable atrocities.
» **Ask** God's help—to grant courage, discernment, and power to pray through His Holy Spirit.
» Then, pray. Pray specifically. Pray, and trust that God hears and intervenes.

Prayer Matter 49

Lord, It Is Night

Do anxious thoughts sometimes keep you awake at night, or maybe awaken you persistently in the wee hours of the morning?

I can understand that happening when I have been lazy in my spiritual life. But even when I try to seek God faithfully by day, my thoughts can have a mind of their own at night. At those times, when I lie down in the dark and the busyness of the day ebbs away, pesky worries enter unbidden into my consciousness and rob me of peaceful sleep.

This is obviously an age-old problem, because it has been addressed in many Scriptures, prayers, songs, and homespun suggestions. The prayer and Scriptures listed are some of these antidotes for fretful sleep.

Try praying them before you lay down to sleep, or when you wake up worrying. When sleep still doesn't come, I suggest just getting up and going to a favorite "prayer closet" to spend some time with your Heavenly Father; He is always awake.

Lord it is night.

The night is for stillness. Let us be still in the presence of God.

It is night after a long day. What has been done has been done; what has not been done has not been done. Let it be.

The night is dark. Let our fears of the darkness of the world and of our own lives rest in You.

The night is quiet. Let the quietness of Your peace enfold us, all dear to us, and all who have no peace.

The night heralds the dawn. Let us look expectantly to a new day, new joys, new possibilities.

In Your name we pray. Amen.

Source: "A New Zealand Prayer Book - He Karakia Mihinare o Aotearoa" – Reprinted with permission.

He will not let your foot slip—He who watches over you will not slumber; indeed, He who watches over Israel will neither slumber nor sleep. *Psalm 121:3–4*

When you lie down, you will not be afraid; when you lie down, your sleep will be sweet. *Proverbs 3:24*

In peace I will lie down and sleep, for You alone, Lord, make me dwell in safety. *Psalm 4:8*

By day the Lord directs His love, at night His song is with me—a prayer to the God of my life. *Psalm 42:8*

For personal reflection and action…

» I keep a copy of the "Lord, It Is Night" prayer by my bedside; the Scriptures shown are printed on the back. Often I read the prayer, Scriptures, or both to direct my thoughts prior to bedtime. I definitely read them whenever I am having trouble at bedtime letting go of the anxieties or busyness of the day.

» Make a practice always to turn your thoughts to God the last thing before closing your eyes to sleep. Say a bedtime prayer. Sometimes I pray a Scripture like Psalm 4:8; sometimes, a bedtime prayer from childhood (See Prayer Matter 37). Other times, Mike and I hold hands and pray a short prayer together. And at times I simply say, "Goodnight, God. I love You. Thank You for loving me."

> "Go to sleep in peace. God is awake."
> *Victor Hugo*

PRAYER MATTER 50

Prayer: Just Do It!

Two devotionals on prayer recently happened across my path in the same day.

In the first, a man attributed changing the way he prayed to God's answering his prayer to save the life of his critically ill child. After reading it, I could not help but ask, "God, had I prayed differently, would You have spared my son's life?"

In the other, a child tearfully asked her parent how prayer works, because what she kept praying for had not come to pass. The parent honestly admitted not understanding how God answers prayers, and I thought, "God, neither do I."

> Then Jesus told his disciples a parable to show them that they ought always to pray and not to faint. *Luke 18:1*

> "The main lesson about prayer is just this: Do it! Do it! DO IT! You want to be taught to pray. My answer is: pray and never faint, and then you shall never fail." *John Laidlaw*

I have a passion for prayer. I have been told, "You are a strong prayer warrior." Trust me, I am not. I have many questions. Although I have read all the Scriptures about prayer, as well as many other resources, there is so much about prayer I do not understand. Too often I fail to practice even that which I do understand about prayer.

> Lord, I wait for You; You will answer, Lord my God. *Psalm 38:15*

In the end, I am left acknowledging that prayer is a profound mystery. So, how can I say it is my passion?

I can say it because Scriptures clearly state that God hears and answers prayer, and I have chosen to believe this. Whenever I have chosen to keep praying, even my poorest efforts have always yielded results.

> Before they call I will answer; while they are still speaking I will hear. *Isaiah 65:24*

Sometimes it is the specific request answered pretty much as asked, occasionally in positive ways I never thought to ask. Often it is a change in my perspective, such as the ability to see blessings in the worst of adversities, or the answer to

> But as for me, I watch in hope for the Lord, I wait for God my Savior; my God will hear me. *Micah 7:7*

a painful question through a Scripture that happens my way, or simply the comforting assurance that God is in control and someday I will understand.

If you, like me, have questions about prayer and how it works, that is just fine. What I would say is, just **do it**. Do it anyway. Do it often. Do it honestly. Take God at His word. Do not faint. Pray.

> "When darkness veils His lovely face, I rest on His unchanging grace." *Edward Mote*

> "More things are wrought by prayer than this world dreams of." *Alfred, Lord Tennyson*

For personal reflection and action...

» Remind yourself that prayer is a profound mystery—a mystery being something that "is," and yet is difficult or impossible to explain.

» **Ask** God to help you. Tell God you trust Him, even though you do not understand the intricate workings of prayer.

» Reflect on Scriptures that confirm the belief in prayer to which Bible characters firmly held. Hold especially close Jesus' teachings about prayer.

» **Ask** God to reveal what He would have you learn about prayer. Be sure to thank God when He grants insight or is gracious to reveal how a prayer has been answered.

» Pray, and keep on praying. I am convinced that in Heaven, we will finally understand how much our prayers have mattered, and how God's grace has covered us throughout all our trials more than we can ever begin to imagine.

About the Author

Marilyn Wragg has enjoyed a rich variety of work experiences. Moving often with her husband Mike in the early years of their marriage, she taught school and worked for an oil company, university, and bank. After settling in Lubbock, she worked thirteen years in sales for General Electric Company. Marilyn then returned to her education roots and served twenty years directing The Curriculum Center for Family and Consumer Sciences at Texas Tech University prior to retiring.

In Marilyn's words, "I retired from full-time work not because I didn't love what I did, but because I wanted more time directly to work for God." That time has primarily been focused in her home church, First Christian Church, Lubbock. Although she volunteers in various areas, prayer is the ministry to which Marilyn most personally feels called.

This book is an outgrowth of that ministry, as it stems from prayer articles written for the church newsletter. After years of developing lessons for public schools, Marilyn's desire is now to share with others some of the lessons God is teaching her about prayer. She writes not as an expert, but as a pilgrim walking alongside those seeking a closer relationship with God.

Marilyn lives in Lubbock, Texas, with her husband, Mike. They are blessed on earth with a married daughter and son-in-law, a daughter-in-law, and three delightful grandchildren, as well as a son who now resides in Heaven.

CPSIA information can be obtained
at www.ICGtesting.com
Printed in the USA
LVOW11s0331131117
556067LV00002B/107/P